The
Goal
and the
Glory

COMPILED BY

Josh Davis
Three-Time Gold Medalist

Regal

From Gospel Light
Ventura, California, U.S.A.

Published by Regal
From Gospel Light
Ventura, California, U.S.A.
www.regalbooks.com
Printed in the U.S.A.

All photos are used by permission by the following organizations and individuals: Josh Davis, Clem Spalding and Craig Harriman; Allyson Felix, © Allyson Felix; Jim Ryun, Jim Ryun Collection; Laura Wilkinson, Ben Chen of Sports Pixel; Jennie Finch, Landon Finch Finch Fotography; Eric Liddell, public domain; Cat Reddick Whitehill, Sideline Sports Photography; Jennifer Barringer, University of Colorado Athletics Department; Brandon Slay, Bill Mulholland; Matt Hemingway, Bryce Boyer Photography; Peter Westbrook, Kmur Hardeman. Other photos provided by Josh Davis. All rights reserved.

Library of Congress Cataloging-in-Publication Data
The goal and the glory : Christian athletes share their inspiring stories / compiled by Josh Davis.
    p. cm.
ISBN 978-0-8307-4600-2 (trade paper)
1. Athletes—Religious life. 2. Sports—Religious aspects—Christianity. I. Davis, Josh.
BV4596.A8G63 2008
248.8'8—dc22
                                                                2008000348

2 3 4 5 6 7 8 9 10 / 14 13 12 11 10 09 08

Rights for publishing this book outside the U.S.A. or in non-English languages are administered by Gospel Light Worldwide, an international not-for-profit ministry. For additional information, please visit www.glww.org, email info@glww.org, or write to Gospel Light Worldwide, 1957 Eastman Avenue, Ventura, CA 93003, U.S.A.

To my best cheerleader and training partner, my wife, Shantel.
To my best coach, my Lord and Savior Jesus Christ.
Thanks for helping me to be more than I could have imagined.

Contents

SECTION TWO: GUTS

SECTION THREE: GLORY

Big Splash

By Max Lucado

Sometime back I took up swimming for exercise. I didn't buy a Speedo, but I did buy some goggles, went to a pool and gave it a go. Over the weeks, I've gradually progressed from a tadpole to a small frog. I'm not much to look at, but I can get up and down the lane. In fact, I was beginning to feel pretty good about my progress.

So good, in fact, that when Josh Davis invited me to swim with him, I accepted. You remember Josh Davis—three-time gold medalist in Atlanta. His waist size is my thigh size. Half his warm-up is my entire workout. He is as comfortable in a swimming lane as most of us are in a cafeteria lane.

So when he offered to give me some pointers, I jumped in the pool. After all, I was over 50 years old with two months of swimming experience under my belt . . . Senior Olympics? Who knows? So with Josh in his lane and me next to him in mine, he suggested, "Swim two laps and let's see how fast you go. I'll be swimming next to you." Off I went. I gave it all I had. I looked up from my thrashing to see him swimming smoothly and splashing less. Onlookers would have thought a torpedo occupied Josh's lane. They would have thought a dying duck swam in mine. He blitzed me. I could have water skied in his wake.

That's why I was surprised at the finish to see that he had touched the wall only seconds before me.

"Have you been here long?" I panted.

"Just nine seconds."

"You mean I finished only nine seconds behind you?"

"That's right."

Whoa! Forget Senior Olympics, I'm thinking Beijing in 2008. But then, Josh added, "There was one difference: While you swam two laps, I swam four."

Josh raised the bar. He elevated the standard. He did, in the pool, what Jesus did for humanity. Jesus demonstrated what a godly life looks like. The best of us will finish laps back in His wake, but still we try. And still we need encouragement.

That's what this book is all about . . . encouragement. Encouragement from great athletes and souls like Josh to do our best to follow the example of Jesus. He sets the pace. And, when we fall short, He provides the grace.

Thanks, Josh, for your example and friendship. May God bless you and all who read this book. And may He teach me how to stay afloat in the pool.

Opening Ceremonies

Josh Davis

Finally! After 10 years and 25,000 miles in training (that's the equivalent of swimming once around the globe), I had arrived at the 1996 Summer Olympics in Atlanta. While I was there to race, I was also there to represent the best country in the world! And I knew deep down it would be one of the biggest tests of my character. At the time I wondered, *Do I have what it takes? Have I prepared enough?*

I am blessed to say that the answer was a resounding yes, both then and at the 2000 Olympics in Sydney! Hi, I'm Josh Davis, two-time Olympian and five-time medalist in swimming—and one of the biggest fans of the Games you've ever met. I love everything about them. I am fascinated by all the competitors from all the countries who train decades for just one race.

If you are even a part-time sports fan, you probably share my fascination with these athletes. I imagine you have watched the Games on TV, wincing when your favorite falls and yelling unabashedly when he or she wins by a hair.

And we all tear up with a smile of gratitude when we hear our national anthem played for "one of ours." They represent not just our country, but also what we admire, what we dream of and what is best about us. The Games are the ultimate reality TV show.

But as fun and inspiring as it is to watch on TV, it's even better being there. In fact, I would be willing to bet that the Olympic Village, where competitors from around the world come to live and train before and during the Games, beats out Disney World as the happiest place on Earth. Why is everybody so happy at the Village? Because everything is free! First, they gave us an overflowing shopping cart full of free red, white and blue clothes. Then we were ushered into a huge arcade with all the latest and greatest video games—and there was even free Lazer Tag! But of course my favorite "freebie" was the free food!! There were a dozen 100-foot-long buffet lanes with all the best food from all around the world. The very sight of it made me declare out loud to my teammate, "I'm in heaven!"

It's a good thing we had those fun free things in the Village, because it was nerve wracking as the competition got closer. Why? I had spent 15 years preparing for the 11 races I competed in between Atlanta and Sydney. And since my races only averaged a minute long, I had spent half my life preparing for just 11 minutes of action. Talk about pressure to perform. But the adrenaline was like no other—and the taste of victory was sweet.

In this book, I'll share some of my favorite moments from the Games in Atlanta and Sydney. I'm so proud to be an athlete who made it to the Olympics. And even more proud to be an American. But I'm busting-at-the-seams proud to be a Christian!

Naturally, I've met many other Christian athletes and am especially moved by their stories. Some are old friends and some are new, but I've interviewed over 30 world-class athletes, from legends Rafer Johnson, John Naber and David Robinson to Ruth Riley, Jenny Barringer and Brooke Abel. The result of these interviews is this devotional, *The Goal and the Glory*. For 60 days, we invite you to delve into the most personal moments of these world-class athletes as you take this behind-the-scenes journey showcasing how they encountered God on their way to glory. At the end of each story, a personal challenge from the athlete pushes you to awaken the greatness in you.

Just as any good journey starts with a goal, so does this book. In "Goals," learn how Olympians made their dreams a reality as they pursued the ultimate goal: discovering who they are in Christ. In "Guts," you'll get an up-close look at the sweat and the passion that goes into making world-class athletes through discipline, preparation, relationships and developing *the X-factor*. These same elements equip us to persevere as disciples of Christ. And finally, in "Glory," we discover what sets these athletes apart from other champions and how we too can please God by fulfilling our purpose.

At the end of the book, I've included interesting sports profiles on each of these world-class athletes that feature their favorite Olympic moments, favorite songs and favorite verses.

PROCESSION

During my interviews with many athletes from around the world, they shared that marching in the opening ceremonies with more than 10,000 other athletes was one of the highlights of their experience. It really cemented in their minds that they had truly made it to the Games as world-class athletes and that marching behind their country's flag was a great honor.

I wish we had processions for new Christians. To have millions of people see your face on TV walking behind Christ's banner of love. It would be forever imprinted in your mind and heart that you represent something much bigger than yourself.

As Christians, we are not alone. We are on a special team, chosen and appointed for a task that God Himself ordained from the very foundations of the world. We need to get excited about our calling and the One who has called us. In Christ, our labor is not in vain, our goal is eternal, and our reward is imperishable.

As you read *The Goal and the Glory*, imagine yourself walking out, carrying Christ's flag. Red for the blood He shed for us, white for the purity and holiness He gives us, and blue for the peace we find in His finished work.

DECLARATION

When the parade of nations stops in the middle of the field in the huge stadium, a booming voice over the loudspeaker calls us to take the Olympic Oath. "We promise to take part in the true spirit of sportsmanship, for the glory of sport and the honor of our country." Next, in unison, we recite the Olympic Creed, written by the modern founder, Baron Pierre De Coubertin:

> The most important thing in the Olympic Games is not to win, but to take part, just as the most important thing in life is not the triumph, but the struggle. The essential thing is not to have conquered, but to have fought well.

It is my prayer that we would take part in the game of life, in the true spirit of love, for the glory of God and for the honor of our Savior.

May this book encourage us to take part in the struggle for holiness as we pursue greatness. May these testimonies remind us that while it is good to be winners in the world's eyes, being winners in God's eyes is far more important.

SECTION ONE

GOALS

Josh Davis

Josh Davis

John Naber

Introduction

Do you know the secret to getting the most out of life? Between meeting job deadlines, juggling car-pool duties and getting the laundry done (again), who has time to think about such questions? When we're young, it's "Get a life." But when we're old, it's "Where did my life go?" So how do we make the most of our time on Earth? How do we know where we're going?

As a motivational speaker, I fly to a different city every week, which means I have this terrible reoccurring problem: I get in my rental car without a clue how to get where I'm going! I usually rely on road maps, but the few times I've had the amazing OnStar system, it has never let me down! It tells me every turn to take and lets me know when I've gotten off course.

Don't you wish we came with a preinstalled spiritual version of the OnStar system? Even though we have the Holy Spirit, wouldn't it be nice to have an angelic little voice whispering unmistakably to you throughout the day? "Oops, be careful. You've gotten off track," or maybe "Good job, you've arrived at your destination!"

What guides you through life? Vague childhood fantasies? The expectations of others? Survival-mode autopilot? Or clear, concrete personal goals? Without a detailed roadmap to personal fulfillment, we merely drift along, getting sidetracked by everyday circumstances. Our lives become a living testimony to the truth of the old saying, "When you aim at nothing, you hit it every time."

The obvious solution to getting the most out of life is to set goals! I agree with the advice of motivational expert Brian Tracy when it comes to success: Write down your goals, make plans to achieve them, and work on your plans every single day.[1]

I don't think he's talking about New Year's resolutions, which each year are often the same as those from the year before. And they wind up abandoned. They are wishful thinking—goals toyed with but never even written down, let alone pursued. In fact, sales and inspiration guru Zig Ziglar laments that 97 percent of people don't have written specific goals for their life.[2]

Maybe that's why we all are so profoundly moved by the drama of the Games, where we meet people who have not only set goals but also *achieved* them. Here are real people with hectic lives, just like ours. They face hardships, setbacks, struggles and disappointments, just like we do. But, somehow, unlike us, they have made their childhood dreams become a reality—and before a global audience! These champions have found the secret to setting goals and really achieving them. Olympians are ordinary people who have made an extraordinary commitment! Genetics may set them apart, and not everyone will be able to reach the heights of athletic glory, but everyone has the potential to be great at something.

God has designed a unique dream for each and every person. So let the moving stories of these world-class athletes awaken the greatness in you. As you become inspired to set personal goals, you will be on the path to becoming the best—the very best—at what God has made you to do and to be!

Notes
1. Brian Tracy, *Goals! How to Get Everything You Want—Faster than You Ever Thought Possible* (CD) (San Francisco: Berrett-Koehler Publishers, Inc., 2003).
2. Zig Ziglar, *Goals: Setting and Achieving Them on Schedule* (CD) (New York: Simon & Schuster Audio, 1996).

1

Contagious Belief

Josh Davis
Three-time U.S. Olympic Gold Medalist in Swimming

Enthusiasm is like a ripple in the water, it grows.
KENNETH GENTLE

During the year prior to the 1996 Olympics, I experienced the biggest slump of my athletic career. As I struggled to juggle training, school, work and my love life—I was trying to figure out how to marry my college sweetheart, Shantel—my swimming game was the worst it had been in years.

At that point in my life, I was so overwhelmed and discouraged that I felt the road to the Games was just too long and hard. I even thought about retiring. Why push so hard for an entire year, only to miss making the team? Why risk experiencing such tremendous disappointment? Still, not knowing what else to do, I decided to show up for practice and begin training.

Providentially, my coach, Kris Kubik, pulled me aside. He said, "I've found a picture of next year's gold medal in the paper today. I've laminated it and it should fit in your wallet. I think you're the best 200-freestyler we've got. Keep this and look at it, because I believe you're going to get one of these gold medals next year! When you get your medal, I want you to give me the picture back."

While I was grateful for the encouragement, I couldn't help but say to myself, *Nice thought, but do you know how hard it is to get one of those?* Statistically, it's easier to win the lottery than it is to win an Olympic gold medal. During the previous Olympic trials, I had choked—and then watched from home in amazement as the 1992 Olympians performed. I wondered, *Do I really have what it takes to do what my heroes have done?*

I wasn't sure of myself, but my coach was. I thought, *He's smart, maybe he knows what he's talking about.* When I realized that he believed in me, I began to believe in myself. And you know what? My first practice went okay. And the next one was a little better. I wasn't the best yet, but I made a decision to train and live as if I were. Soon I was in a groove, executing my daily schedule and practicing like the best 200-freestyler in the country. I was living out my dream, one stroke at a time.

When Kubik believed I could be a gold medalist, I began to act like one. When I returned from Atlanta, I showed Kubik not only one but *three* gold medals—and I gave him a hug. Then I gave him back his picture and said, "Thanks for believing in me!"

In the same way that my coach believed in me, God believes in us—in who we are in Him. Remember, God has assured us that we are forgiven, saved and adopted into His family—He has given us a new identity (see 2 Cor. 5:17). We only need to accept His grace to start living the abundant life He has called us to.

If you're in a slump and looking for motivation, consider your true self, the person that God wants you to be. Ask yourself whether you are living out your new identity in Christ. Until you do, you cannot enter into the amazing future God has in store.

> *Therefore, if anyone is in Christ, he is a new creation;*
> *the old has gone, the new has come!*
> 2 Corinthians 5:17

2

Legacy of Champions

Jeremy Knowles
Bahamian Olympic Swim Team

*Who you are and what you do with your life can have
an impact on others for generations to come.*

DENNIS RAINEY

Being an athlete and competitor is in my blood—literally. If I compete in Beijing in 2008, members of my family will have either competed or coached in the Games for the past 60 years (with the exception of the 1980 boycott). My grandfather, Percival Knowles, made four sailing teams. His brother, Durward, made eight sailing teams and was the oldest competitor ever when he competed in the 1988 Olympics at age 70. My cousin, Randy, was a reserve crewman in the 1972 Olympics. At the 1976 Games, my dad, Andy Knowles, and my Uncle Bruce were the first Bahamians ever to compete in swimming.

As a kid, I sat fascinated for hours listening to the legendary adventures of my grandfather and his brother. Great-Uncle Durward always loved retelling his quest for the bronze medal at the 1956 Olympics and then later capturing the 1964 gold medal.

They shared their agonies as well. Once, Grandfather Percival and Uncle Durward were in the running for a bronze when their mast broke, and they finished fifth instead.

My dad and uncle also taught me practical things, like how to prepare, race, represent my country with pride, and make the most of the experience. Growing up as a Knowles, I always felt like an athletic superstar, even though I hadn't yet earned the privilege of being one.

So from an early age, I always loved getting in the pool to train. In fact, the worst punishment my parents could give me as a child was not allowing me to work out. After the heartbreak of barely missing qualifying for the 1996 Games, I eventually made the 2000 Olympic team in Sydney when I was 18, and then continued the tradition at Athens.

While I'm grateful for the legacy my family modeled for me, their spiritual heritage has been even more important in my life. Despite being sporting legends in the Bahamas, members of my family always made their relationship with Jesus their top priority. Because of their faith, I grew up watching my parents always treat people right, persevere through trials and live a life of real integrity. At the 2004 Olympics in Athens, my dad, as the Bahamian swim coach, led a daily Bible study for our delegation. He and Jesus are my models for how to live life to the fullest.

They say what is modeled for you has an incredible impact on your life. I knew from a very young age that being a Knowles was something special, and I wanted to live up to our family name. In our Christian life, it's also important to remember who we are and the One we represent. We are God's children, part of God's family, forgiven and freed by His grace, sealed for eternity in His kingdom.

How well are you modeling your heavenly Father's character? What legacy are you leaving? Remember, you have a God-given goal to be your best, shining for Him!

I pray also that the eyes of your heart may be enlightened in order that you may know the hope to which he has called you, the riches of his glorious inheritance in the saints, and his incomparably great power for us who believe.
EPHESIANS 1:18-19

God's Masterpiece

Madeline Manning Mims
U.S. Olympic Gold Medalist in Track

*Like the genetic code that describes your unique passions and abilities,
your Big Dream has been woven into your being from birth.
You're the only person with a Dream quite like yours.*
BRUCE WILKINSON

When I was in high school, I compared myself to the "cool gang."
They had a certain sway in their walk, were influential, stuck together and set the rules for the majority. Perhaps because I was
somewhat introverted, I wasn't invited to be a part of their popular clique.

When President John F. Kennedy launched the Presidential
Physical Fitness Program to compare American children's physical fitness to children around the world, I surprisingly scored very
high and started setting national standards in my age group.
Before I knew it, I found myself playing on my school's basketball, volleyball and track teams. All three of my teams won state
championships before I graduated. I think I had something to do
with that!

Until my hidden talent for sport was discovered, I was totally
unaware of the athletic gifts inside me. I couldn't even conceive of
the possibility of ever winning a gold medal—or setting American
and World records.

But God knew. Before anyone else knew of my existence, God was working in secret to make me into the person He wanted me to be (see Psalm 139:15-16). What this psalm says to me is that God fashioned and designed me to be a runner. These long legs, big feet and slim build were meant to glorify Him. And I do that by being what He made me to be: an athlete.

I will boast in being His masterpiece, His workmanship created to do good works that please the Master Designer.

> *Father, I am created in Your image and Your*
> *likeness for one purpose in the earth and that is to be*
> *what You have created me to be and bring glory*
> *to Your name. My life is Yours to design*
> *in the beauty of Your holiness in Christ Jesus. Amen.*

God created you in His image and likeness, with special abilities. What has God uniquely fashioned into your DNA? Is there something He's prepared you to do?

What keeps you awake at night with excitement?

What did you enjoy doing as a child?

What are you passionate about?

What is something you've always been good at?

What fulfills you?

Reflect on who God has made you to be—and you will discover your purpose.

> *For we are God's workmanship, created in Christ Jesus to do good works,*
> *which God prepared in advance for us to do.*
> EPHESIANS 2:10

4

Goals to Grow By

Congressman Jim Ryun
U.S. Olympic Silver Medalist in the 1500-Meter Run

How am I going to live today in order to create the
tomorrow I'm committed to?
ANTHONY ROBBINS

By the spring of 1963, I emerged from being a nameless sopho-more who couldn't finish workouts to one of Kansas's top high school milers. It didn't take long for both Coach Timmons ("Tim-mie") and me to realize I was born to run.

One day on the long bus ride from Kansas City back home to Wichita, Timmie talked to me about goals. I had just sloshed my way to a 4:21 mile on a very wet cinder track. "What do you think you can run this year?" Coach Timmons asked.

"This season?" I replied. Before he could answer, I said, "I don't know—maybe 4:15."

He nodded. "I think you can go much faster. How fast do you think you can run before you graduate?"

I thought for a minute. I knew Archie San Romani, a former Wichita East runner, held the national record at 4:08. "Maybe 4:07?" I guessed.

Out came Timmie's pencil and pad, so I knew he was in earnest.

"Jim," he said, turning in his seat to look at me, "I think you can break Archie's record. In fact, I think you can be the first high school boy under 4 minutes for the mile."

I was surprised. I was new to the sport of running, but I knew that only nine years earlier Roger Bannister had been the first man ever to break four minutes for a mile. I know the shock registered on my face, but Coach Timmons kept talking. He explained that it would take hard work, two workouts a day, and long weekend runs of 18 to 20 miles. I wasn't fully convinced at first, but I came to the conclusion that if Coach Timmons believed I could do it, then I could.

I learned a lot of life lessons from Coach Timmons. One of the most valuable was how to set goals. He always had his runners make two sets of goals: short-term (what we wanted to achieve that year) and long-term (what our ultimate goal was in running as well as in life). Timmie had us write down our goals so that they were in front of us—and our teammates—at all times.

Goal-setting can help in our spiritual lives, too. One of our short-term goals should be to be more like Christ. And of course, our long-term goal is heaven.

I encourage you to write down goals for yourself, not only for your professional career, but also for your family and for your spiritual walk. Do you want to increase your productivity at work? Set some time-management goals. Do you want to be healthier? Set some physical-fitness goals. Do you want better quiet time in the morning? Set a goal of 15 to 20 minutes every morning reading God's Word and turning to Him in prayer.

What other goals do you have? Go ahead, write them down today. As you run down this path of life, echo the words of the apostle Paul:

Therefore I run thus: not with uncertainty. Thus I fight: not as one who beats the air. But I discipline my body and bring it into subjection, lest, when I have preached to others, I myself should become disqualified.
1 CORINTHIANS 9:26-27, *NKJV*

Search for Significance

Barb Lindquist
U.S. Swimmer and Olympic Triathlete

We have two alternatives: We can base our self-worth on our success and ability to please others, or we can base our self-worth on the love, forgiveness and acceptance of Christ.
ROBERT S. MCGEE

As a great athlete, it's easy to define myself by my accomplishments: "Stanford swimmer, No. 1 in the world, Olympian." It's been a continual struggle to find my identity from Christ rather than from my race performances.

Growing up, my identity came from being a fast swimmer and straight-A student. As a member of the U.S. National Swim Team, I medaled in two Pan Am Games and one Pan Pacific Games. Attending Stanford University on a swimming scholarship, I made the Dean's list all but one quarter during my four years there.

My last year of swimming, I dreaded competitions because I raced with the fear of failure. When I performed poorly, I felt down.

In 1991, I graduated from college and retired from swimming. After moving to Jackson, Wyoming, I realized I had lost my identity of champion swimmer and great student. Jackson didn't have a competition pool, and I wasn't a student anymore. Waiting tables at night and gaining weight, I struggled with my self-worth, even though as a Christian, I knew better. In my head, I knew that in Christ I was loved and worthy; in my heart, I didn't feel it.

After a few years trying new athletic endeavors and failing, God broke me. Physically and mentally tired from trying to get my inner kudos from what I did, God revealed to me finally that He loved me regardless of my performance. If I ran 8 miles or none that day, if I weighed 150 pounds or 125 pounds, it didn't matter—His love was unconditional. What a freedom that was to know His love for me was not based on how I looked or raced. God brought stability to my life, despite the ups and downs of being an elite athlete.

And God birthed a new desire to race again. With a new freedom, I began racing because I wanted to, not because I needed to. I dabbled in triathlons just for fun.

As an added bonus, I met my future husband, Loren, on a cycling club ride. He encouraged me to turn professional. In April 1996, I entered my first professional race on our honeymoon, just a week after our wedding. Team Lindquist was born.

With my identity anchored in Christ, I look forward to triathlons because I'm excited to discover what God is going to do through me on race day. It brings me great joy and honor when I step up to the line. With my self-worth secure in God, it totally takes the pressure off racing and makes it fun. Amazingly, God has used me as much in losses—like the disappointment of not making the 2000 Olympic team—as in wins . . . even though I still prefer the wins! Now it's my greatest desire to use the talents God has given me to glorify Him, not me.

Where does your sense of value and personal worth come from? Are you basing your self-worth on your performance, or on God's unconditional love for you?

But when the kindness and love of God our Savior appeared,
he saved us, not because of righteous things we had done, but
because of his mercy.
TITUS 3:4-5

Choosing God's Dream

Laura Wilkinson
U.S. Olympic Gold Medalist in Diving

I'm surrendering my Dream to you, Dream Giver.
I've decided that it's You that I can't go on without.
"ORDINARY" IN *THE DREAM GIVER*

At the 2004 Olympic trials, I really struggled. As the defending Olympic gold medalist and current World Cup Platform Champion, everyone had high expectations for a repeat, especially me. In my first Trials event, the pressure, coupled with my wrist injury, proved to be too much. My synchronized-diving partner, Kimiko, and I didn't make the Olympic team. For my individual competition, I was determined to turn things around—but the pressure just continued to mount.

Trailing behind in points with only two dives left, I listened to "I Will Walk by Faith" by one of my favorite singers, Jeremy Camp. The song is his proclamation to walk by faith even when he can't see what God is doing. He reflects on how broken roads prepare us for God's better plan. The words just hit me like a ton of bricks. I had been trying to make the team on my own strength.

That song also reminded me of the book *The Dream Giver* by Bruce Wilkinson, which I had read the year before. In this modern-day parable, the main character, Ordinary, entrusts his dream to God. I realized that I had been trying to reach my dream in my way instead of giving it to God and following His plan for my life.

I confessed, "God, I'm sorry that I've been following my own dreams. I realize that trusting You means I have to give up my dreams to You, but I know that You have plans for me far greater than I could ever imagine. Take my dream, God!"

That was a turning point. God gave me peace that everything would be okay, regardless of the outcome. God chose to bless me with a final dive that secured my spot on the Olympic team.

At the 2004 Olympic Games, my performance was merely average. Sure, I was a little disappointed because my goal had been to win, but I put my heart on the line and fought with everything I had. This time, though, God said no. But I still felt strangely complete. Afterward, I disappointed the reporters by not being a bitter or sore loser. Instead, I shared this: "I came here to glorify God, and that's what I did."

Following wrist surgery the next year, my passion for diving miraculously returned. Then God blessed me by allowing me to win the 2005 World Championship.

Even as I mature in my walk with God, I still struggle with control. But it's my heart's cry that I won't get in God's way—that I'll always choose His will over mine, even when I don't understand.

What dreams do you need to give to Him? Even when you can't see what God is doing, I encourage you to walk by faith, knowing that God is always faithful to all of His promises.

Many are the plans in a man's heart, but it is the
Lord's purpose that prevails.
PROVERBS 19:21

I will instruct you and teach you in
the way you should go; I will
counsel you and watch over you.
PSALM 32:8

Trusting God's Approach

Matt Hemingway
U.S. Olympic Silver Medalist in High Jump

"He knows the way He taketh," even if for the moment we do not.
J. I. PACKER

After retiring from professional high jumping in June 1997, I started working as a sales manager for U.S. West Communications and enjoyed playing basketball with the guys during lunch. Two years later, I discovered our company also sponsored a corporate track team, and I decided to try jumping again just for fun. I shocked everyone, including myself, when I jumped 7' on my first attempt. Before long I cleared 7' 4", a first for a practice jump.

Two months later, I qualified for the National Championships. That year I set three personal records and even had the highest indoor jump in the world at 7' 9". Amazingly, I won the 2000 U.S. Indoor Championship while still working over 50 hours a week in sales management.

This astonishing comeback suddenly thrust me back into the international scene, so my expectations for the Sydney Olympics were high. However, at the U.S. Olympic trials in Sacramento, I experienced one of the worst meets of my life and didn't make the team. I struggled for two months, questioning why God allowed me to come out of retirement and jump so high, only to fall short of making our team.

Tired and frustrated, I called my dad, a lieutenant colonel in the Marines, who has always been someone I've looked up to for spiritual guidance. Dad always said, "He is . . . and I'm His." I called him from Europe to get some advice and left a message on his answering machine asking him to call. Forgetting it was only 3 A.M. in Monaco, Dad called back, waking my wife, Kate, and me. After a 45-minute heart-to-heart talk, I asked him what he thought I should do.

"What does Kate think?" Dad asked.

I wearily replied, "She's ready to come home, too."

"Whenever you and your wife are in agreement, it's a good place to start making decisions," Dad wisely advised.

"Thanks, Dad. We'll be home in a couple of days," I said as I hung up, not yet realizing the significance of that conversation. After a few more hours of sleep, we got up and made arrangements to head back to the United States.

Only God knew that within five minutes of our flight landing in Denver, my dad would suffer a major heart attack and go to be with the Lord. I now understood God's perfect timing. He had intervened, without forcing me to make a choice between going to the Games and attending my father's funeral.

It's natural to question God during trials. But my Sydney disappointment reminds me that even when we don't understand, God sees the entire picture and always has our best interest at heart.

Is there an area in your life where you're still questioning the outcome? I challenge you to trust God, knowing that He's always one jump ahead.

And I am sure that God who began the good work
within you will keep right on helping you grow in his
grace until his task within you is finally finished
on that day when Jesus Christ returns.
PHILIPPIANS 1:6, TLB

Changing Seasons

Vonetta Flowers
U.S. Olympic Gold Medalist in Bobsledding

*If we are afraid of the future, afraid of change, then we will
miss out on what God has called us to do.*
CONGRESSMAN JIM RYUN

I trained most of my life for the Summer Olympics, so becoming the first African-American ever to win a gold medal in the Winter Olympics seemed unimaginable. But looking back on my journey, I realize that God had the perfect plan from the start.

My husband, Johnny, jokes a lot, so when he brought up the idea of us trying out for the bobsled teams together, I didn't know whether to take him seriously or laugh. Johnny hadn't trained at an elite level since college, four years earlier, so I knew he was serious when he purchased track spikes.

After days of listening to his begging and pleading, I reluctantly agreed to accompany Johnny to the U.S. Bobsled Team tryouts. Soon after the competition began, Johnny pulled his hamstring and somehow managed to convince me to live out his dream. Without his encouragement, my bobsled career would have been over before it started.

I knew absolutely nothing about bobsleds. All of my "bobsled knowledge" came from watching the movie *Cool Runnings*, so you can imagine my surprise when I actually made the team. I hoped that I would be able to transfer the skills gained as a sprinter and long jumper into my new sport. Even with those skills, I still didn't know exactly what to expect. But, after agreeing to fly to Germany, I was ready for my first bobsled ride. All I remember is praying the entire time and holding on for dear life. God alone knew what my future held, and He also knew that given the chance, I would use those skills to honor Him.

The only thing holding me back from being successful was the bulk of the 450-pound bobsled. Once I started a serious weight-training program, I gained the necessary strength and excelled at my new sport. In 2002, my partner Jill Bakken and I entered the history books, winning the first-ever U.S. gold medal in Women's Bobsled. Although the media considered it an upset of monumental proportions, our victory was no surprise to my Creator.

As I mature as a Christian, I am learning that God's plans will ultimately take us out of our comfort zone. We must only be willing to change course and follow where He leads. I am amazed by the number of doors that have opened because of my willingness to step out in faith. While I was chasing my dreams of competing in the Summer Olympics, God had already destined me to be a Winter Olympian so that I could inspire and encourage others to reach the goals that God has for them.

I believe that for significant growth to take place, we must be willing to move out of our comfort zone and be willing to follow where God leads us. In what area is God asking you to step out of your comfort zone in faith?

See, I am doing a new thing!
Now it springs up; do you not perceive it?
I am making a way in the desert and
streams in the wasteland.
Isaiah 43:19

9

Choosing Wisely

LaVonna Martin-Floreal
U.S. Olympic Silver Medalist in 100-Meter Hurdles

Christianity is not a solo sport.
DAVID EDWARDS

Although I made a decision for Christ as a child, looking back I realize that for much of my athletic career, I tried putting God in a box. I prayed for what I wanted instead of seeking God's will. Regretfully, I even put my relationship with God on the shelf when it wasn't useful or convenient, dabbling in things that I knew weren't right.

After making it to the finals in the 1988 Olympics, my eye was on a medal for 1992. When the opportunity came to train with a top coach, I said a quick prayer, but I didn't seek godly counsel before I left my college coach. Under the direction of my new coach, my hard work paid off—in 1990, I earned the No. 1 American female ranking in the 100-meter hurdles.

But my world came crashing down in January 1991 when I mysteriously failed a drug test. I couldn't believe it! I knew there had to be a mistake, because I would never cheat to win. While I maintained my innocence, an investigation was launched. I felt utterly betrayed when my new coach admitted she had been giving me an illegal substance without my knowledge.

In 1991, my Olympic dreams ended after the governing body suspended me from all competition for two years. However, they offered a glimmer of hope by labeling me an "innocent victim" of my coach and recommending that I apply for early reinstatement.

It would have been easy to sink into a deep pit of self-pity, but my suspension marked a major turning point in my life. Realizing I needed to change, I moved back home where my family and church family surrounded me with unconditional love and support. They insisted I get involved in church and Bible study. They also kept interceding in prayers on my behalf during this tough time. They encouraged me to stay in top condition on my own.

Just two months before the 1992 Olympic trials, my ban was lifted and I went back to train with my college coach. But this time, I had my priorities in order. During my suspension, I had learned something invaluable: Instead of racing to beat a competitor, winning the applause of the crowd or pleasing my coaches, my performance was now for an audience of one—God.

When I made the Olympic team in 1992, I knew it was nothing short of a miracle! At the Barcelona Olympics, my trials turned into triumph. Not only did I win the silver medal, but I also met my future husband. Through my ordeal, I learned the importance of community and mentorship. Now I regularly surround myself with older godly women who coach me about everyday life. Unfortunately, most young people aren't taught the value of connecting with wise, experienced people. It's so smart to seek advice from others who have character—and who have already accomplished what you want to do.

Is God your Head Coach and your first source of counsel? Do you seek confirmation from others who are grounded in biblical principles? If you don't already have a mentor, I challenge you to pray for one. Then seek someone you respect who has successfully traveled down the path you desire to go and ask if you can travel alongside them.

To God belong wisdom and power; counsel and understanding are his.
JOB 12:13

10

Energizing Compass

Josh Davis
Three-time U.S. Olympic Gold Medalist in Swimming

Never look down to test the ground before taking your next step; only he who keeps his eye fixed on the far horizon will find his right road.
DAG HAMMARSKJOLD

My sophomore year at Winston Churchill High School was incredible. That year, at the 1988 Texas State Championship Meet, I won my first individual title, the coveted team title and a relay title, on top of being named team MVP. Since I was only 15 and had completed just 2 years of rigorous training, I thought I was doing pretty well. By the end of that year, I was ready to kick back and enjoy a little break.

But Coach Al Marks wouldn't let us rest on our laurels. He sat the relay team down and gave us our goals for the next state meet, 12 months later. The paper he gave us simply read, "4x100 Free Relay National Record—3:02:61." Now this record was held by an elite private school, and we were an ordinary public high school. But he encouraged us: If each of us on the team dropped just one second, we could break the record.

Now, a one-second drop is quite an accomplishment, and to do it in one year is impressive indeed. However, it was a risky commitment for us. As part of a four-man relay team, each of us knew there was always the chance that maybe one of us wouldn't be as dedicated as the others. We were only as strong as our weakest link.

Still, seeing the time on the piece of paper did something. Nothing mystical or magical happened, but something powerful was in the air. Now we had direction. We had something that gave us an adrenaline boost. It was an energizing compass that helped us evaluate every decision we made: *Does that get me closer to my goal? Does this distract me from my goal?* The goal time on that little piece of paper motivated us to do the little things right, pushing through pain barriers and obstacles.

After a whole year, it was finally time for the race. Our strategy was to set the record right away in the prelims and be done with it. Sadly, we missed it by exactly two-tenths of a second, so we had to regroup and find more energy for the finals the next day.

With only one chance left to break the record after a year of preparation, we should have been stressed. But focusing on the goal time got us excited instead of anxious. Finally, the moment had arrived.

Not only did we break the record, but it still stands today, 19 years later!

I am forever grateful that Coach Marks taught me about goal setting while I was still in high school. I learned firsthand that goals allow us to accomplish things we couldn't achieve before: All four of us won our individual events, we won the team title again, and we were voted best high school team in the country!

A great coach is someone who believes in you and teaches you how to operate at your very best. Who are the people in your daily life who are "coaching" you? There is no better Coach than the One who designed you. Is God calling you to something greater? Pray about where God wants you to be a year from now.

> *You guide me with your counsel, and afterward*
> *you will take me into glory.*
> PSALM 73:24

11

Not "Ida" but "I Am"

Brandon Slay
U.S. Olympic Gold Medalist in Wrestling

*Failure is, in a sense, the highway to success, since every discovery of
what is false leads us to seek earnestly after what is true.*

JOHN KEATS

Are you living up to your full potential as an athlete and as a person? Jesus said He came into the world to give us life in all its fullness (see John 10:10). Is that the kind of life you have? Sadly, lots of people don't, but they always seem to have some excuse.

I don't know how many times through the years I've heard someone give me an "Ida." You know, "I would have . . ."

"Ida had a better life, but I hung out with the wrong crowd."

"Ida been successful, but I failed my classes."

"Ida graduated from college, but I partied too much with alcohol and drugs."

Sportspeople are no exception. I know so many athletes who had great potential in high school, but they wasted it by making bad choices. Then all they can say is, "Ida won state, if Ida been more committed."

"Ida wrestled in college, if Ida put more time in."

"Ida won National and World titles, if only Ida really made up my mind to work hard to develop my talent."

Trust me, I was no angel throughout my 19-year journey to the Games. I made lots of bad choices and stumbled badly because of them. But early on in sports, I learned the importance of turning stumbling blocks into stepping-stones.

Of course, that's just what Jesus does with our spiritual lives. A year before the 2000 Games, I had to admit I wasn't proud of the selfish, impure, angry man I had become. But the Jesus whom I had learned about as a child would not let me go. When I decided to lean on Him as a man, I watched Him change my spiritual stumbling blocks into inner-strength-building stepping-stones. As a Christian, I learned:

- I am chosen and set apart (see Ephesians 1:4).
- I am accepted and worthy (see Romans 15:7; Psalm 139).
- I am seen as perfect (see Hebrews 10:14; Colossians 2:13).
- I am adequate (see Corinthians 3:5-6; Philippians 4:13).
- I am bold and confident (see Proverbs 3:26; 14:26; Hebrews 10:19).
- I am filled with hope (see Romans 15:13; Psalm 33:17-18).[1]

Confident in Christ, I could now face failure with hope for the future, instead of anger about the past. Of course, that's the key to becoming a champion. In sports, you don't learn how to do everything well on the first try. You need the staying power to keep trying long enough until you figure out how to do it right.

In Sydney, things didn't go smoothly, but I always knew who I was in Christ. No one could take away that confidence and hope that He had given me. Because of Jesus, I was able to fail my way to an Olympic gold medal!

How do you handle your flaws and failures? Do you run from them with "Idas"? Or face them knowing who you are in Christ?

But he said to me, "My grace is sufficient for you,
for my power is made perfect in weakness."
2 CORINTHIANS 12:9

Note
1. Neil Anderson, *Who I Am in Christ* (Ventura, CA: Regal Books, 2001), p. 278.

12

Sole Supplier

Madeline Manning Mims
U.S. Olympic Gold Medalist in Track

I need God more than anything I might get from God.
PHILLIP YANCEY

Something I've noticed in life about God: He rarely uses us when we're feeling adequate (i.e., prayed up, fasted up, feeling strong in our faith, rested and ready for battles in life). Instead, He often calls us when we are unsure, scared, weak, doubtful, broke and beaten down. In my experience, only when we have reached this place of utter dependence does God act to take us to the next level of maturity and influence. I always wondered about this backward-seeming process, so I prayed and listened.

He answered me: "I want you to see Me as your Sole Supplier":

- Trust Me with all your heart (see Proverbs 3:5).
- Let your faith grow (see Hebrews 11:1,6).
- Commit yourself to Me (see Psalm 37:5).
- Brokenness involves dying to yourself to live for Me (see Psalm 51:1-3,7-10).
- Acknowledge Me first in all things (see Proverbs 3:6).
- Desire to please Me (see Esther 7:3).
- Know that I am your Lord who provides openly for you (see Luke 12:22-32).
- Remember I have a plan for your life (see Jeremiah 29:11).

- Look to Me to give you daily bread (see Matthew 6:11).
- Know that My love never fails, no matter what
  (see 1 John 4:16-18).

When I have plenty or if I'm struggling, it's my prayer that I'll always have a heart that's thankful to God. Sometimes God cuts all our support systems to bring us to a place of total dependency on Him. Surrendering to God's will is difficult, but it's so much better than putting our faith in temporary things that won't satisfy.

Are you acknowledging God as your Sole Supplier? What needs are you trying to meet on your own that you need to surrender to God? Remember that He has good and perfect gifts waiting for you. Honor God by thanking Him in advance for supplying everything according to His riches in glory.

I know what it is to be in need, and I know what it is to have plenty.
I have learned the secret of being content in any and every situation,
whether well fed or hungry, whether living in plenty or in want.
PHILIPPIANS 4:12

But my God shall supply all your need according to
his riches in glory by Christ Jesus.
PHILIPPIANS 4:19, *KJV*

Every good and perfect gift is from above,
coming down from the Father of the heavenly lights,
who does not change like shifting shadows.
JAMES 1:17

Conclusion

What can we learn from these inspiring stories? It's what every accomplished athlete, top business leader or motivational expert will tell you: Setting goals is critical for achieving success. But goal setting isn't limited to our earthly ambitions. While my high school coaches had taught me how to set goals, work hard and lead by example, I was still missing something.

In 1991, as a college freshman, my life forever changed: Darin McFarland with Athletes in Action explained to me how I could daily grow closer to Jesus Christ and enter into the abundant life He wanted me to live. He made it clear that our Lord wanted to save me—and had always been at work, enabling me to fulfill His goals for my life.

Darin taught me that God knew all about setting goals. Because Jesus, God's Son, understood His goal—to bring salvation to the world—He stayed amazingly focused. He knew He had come into this world to die and make the Great Exchange—to take away our sins and replace them with His perfect relationship with the Father. So when Peter told Him there must be another way, Jesus said, "Get behind me, Satan!" (Matthew 16:23). Clearly, self-help gurus didn't invent the concepts of setting goals, persevering and striving for excellence—God did.

The testimonies of these world-class athletes bear out the reality that as Christians, we need to follow the lead of the ultimate Head Coach when it comes to setting our goals.

1. *Make a written list.* Habakkuk 2:2 tells us to write the vision down. Having our goals always in front of us helps keeps us focused and committed. I'm a fan of motivational speaker Lewis Timberlake, who always

challenges his audiences: "Take a circle, draw an 'x' in it and then a line down the middle. That should make six pie pieces within the circle. Those pie pieces represent the six areas of your life you should have goals in: professional, social, family, physical, mental and spiritual."

2. *Discern your God-given purpose.* It was a lightbulb moment when I realized that long before I was born, God designed me to fulfill specific goals as a part of His plan for the world (see Psalm 139:16). Inner satisfaction does not come from just setting good goals you want to achieve, but from discovering and fulfilling God's goals for you. As my pastor, Max Lucado, puts it, find your "sweet spot"—the job or life-calling you were created for—the zone, region, life precinct in which you were made to dwell. Let your unique God-given design determine your goals in life.

3. *Have a support system.* It's good to know He has given us everything we need to accomplish what He has set aside for us to do, even a supportive community (see 2 Peter 1:3; 2 Corinthians 9:8; Ephesians 2:10). I know that having my teammates pushing me every day in practice made a big difference in my development. Likewise, having Christian mentors walk beside us gives us the grace and encouragement we need to push through the obstacles we will encounter as we seek to achieve our goals.

What's the secret to achieving your dreams? Following God's goals for you in the power of His Holy Spirit and in the company of His people. In this "sweet spot," you'll find the energy and direction you need to get past all the disappointments and difficulties that stand between you and the fulfillment of your unique calling.

Insights into the Heart of a Champion

Rev. Canon Dr. John Ashley Null
Two-time Olympic Chaplain

The athletic dream says that all your problems will fade away if you can just make it to the top—the very top—of your sport. In reality, many elite athletes find themselves deeply disappointed when they get there. Unlike the vast majority of sportspeople who never make it to that level, champions learn firsthand the hard truth that superior athletic success, by itself, won't make you happy. If you are miserable on the inside before you win an Olympic medal, you will still be miserable afterward. A medal outside doesn't change what's on the inside.

Sporting success cannot solve your personal problems. If you fail to develop yourself as a person while you develop yourself as an athlete, you are simply building castles in the sand. When the storms of life beat against you, everything you've worked for comes tumbling down.

Why isn't winning enough? It's quite simple, really: God designed human beings to need Him in their lives. Only His unconditional love in our hearts gives us a sense of self-worth that won't go away.

Without God in our lives, we are trapped into using our talent to find some reason to like ourselves. We expect our accomplishments to make us feel good about who we are. But God has reserved this role for Himself alone. As a result, we always tend to be disappointed by the results of our own achievements. And because we often overlook the needs of others in our pursuit of success, we can easily also end up alone.

Athletes are no exception. Most go through life expecting to feel good about themselves as long as they are winning and the crowd is shouting its approval. They are soon disappointed, however. It doesn't take long to discover that the thrill of victory is so very short-lived. But because they have learned to think that achievement is the only way to be fulfilled, top athletes stay on the treadmill. They tell themselves that the fame, fortune and easy short-term relationships that come with being a sports star are the hallmarks of the best possible life. So they keep straining for the next accomplishment, hoping that it will make them feel truly content. But they remain deeply unsatisfied. They may be winners in sport, but they're surely losing out on life.

Why do such incredibly talented people get trapped on this treadmill? For the same reason it happens to everyone else: The spiritual enemy of humanity is always trying to psych each one of us out of trusting God's love. Here's how he does it:

- Step 1: *He tries to plant a negative attitude in you.* His method is to get you to concentrate on what you don't have rather than on what you do.

- Step 2: *The enemy makes you doubt that God loves you.* You don't look for love from someone who mistreats you, so humanity's enemy tries to make God look unfair for not giving you all that you desire.

- Step 3: *He undermines your self-esteem for who you are now.* Once the enemy has got you to doubt God's love for you, he is able to get you to doubt yourself. How does he do it? He just compares you to others. It's effective, because in this life no one has it all.

- Step 4: *The enemy convinces you to work for your self-worth.* With God out of the picture, it's up to you to find a way to feel "good enough" about yourself. You may not measure up right now, but you can some day, if you will only use your abilities to make yourself a success.

- Step 5: *The enemy's lie makes you its slave.* When you live life without God's love, you try to satisfy your heart with the self-love that comes from success. But the thrill of each achievement fades too quickly, so you start looking ahead to the next chance to get ahead. And the more you succeed, the more you find yourself a slave.

Christian athletes, however, take a different approach. They look at the vast expanse of the universe, governed by discernible laws (not chaos), and they see an architect—God. They look at their own bodies, how ingeniously the human anatomy has been designed, and they see the handiwork of their Maker. They look into their heart, feel a longing for love and see the fingerprints of a God who so greatly desires to have a relationship with them that He created them to desire what He alone can give. Having the guts to step off the treadmill, these athletes decide to stop living for sport alone and begin to learn about the Source of life.

They look into the Bible and recognize that what God has said about human nature is true, and they admit it's true about them, too. They acknowledge that, despite all their best accomplishments, they can't find fulfillment on their own. They realize that despite all their best intentions, their pursuit of self-worth often causes them to hurt others in the process. They look into the Bible, they recognize that Jesus is trustworthy, and they lean on God's promises for forgiveness and new life through Christ.

In Jesus, Christian athletes find their greatest fulfillment. Because of Him, they don't have to misuse sport by trying to earn self-love through it. They know Jesus' love gives them a worth that will never go away.

Not misusing sport to prove their importance or solve their problems, Christian athletes can once again enjoy:

- the physical rush that comes from pushing their body to its limits;

- meaningful relationships with other sportspeople, even competitors;

- a reputation for having strong character and a well-balanced personality.

In sum, because Jesus has enabled them to achieve real joy in life, Christian athletes can recover real joy in sport.

What about you? Have you been psyched out of trusting God's love? Have you lost your joy at the office or at home, or even both, because you feel you have something to prove? Are you a slave to having to be better than other people? Do you need Jesus to do for you what He has done for all the athletes whose testimonies you have read in this book?

To be the very best God's unconditional love can make you. To feel the Father's arms around your neck. To hear God Almighty say in your ear, "Well done, My good and faithful child. Share My joy, real joy, forever." That gold-medal ceremony awaits everyone who trusts in Jesus.

Adapted from Ashley Null, *Real Joy: Freedom to Be Your Best* (Germany: Ebner & Spiegel, Ulm, 2004). Used by permission.

SECTION TWO

GUTS

Allyson Felix

John Register

Jim Ryun

Laura Wilkinson

Introduction

Discipline is one of the most hated terms of our times . . . right alongside patience and self-control. But have you noticed how often it comes up in the testimonies of those who win?

CHUCK SWINDOLL

I'd be lying to you if I said that over the course of the million laps I swam in my 15 years of Olympic training, I never got discouraged, tempted or distracted. To be honest there were many days when I wanted to slack off or even skip practice. It would have been easy to get off course by pursuing girls, watching movies or making a career of social functions. And it definitely would have been *a lot more fun!* There was always a temptation to stay out late with my buddies instead of disciplining myself to get up at 5:45 A.M.

In this next section, the Olympians will share their stories of the obstacles they had to overcome. We've all faced them: injuries, being overwhelmed by all the hard work ahead, the temptation to take an easier road, distractions of life (good and bad), the disillusionment of slumps, the discouragement of feeling alone, or the frustration of bad communication between coach and athlete, boss and employee. At one time or another, we've all wanted to quit.

Winston Churchill, the great Prime Minister of England during World War II, and my high school's namesake, understood the temptation to give up. In the face of the massive Nazi military machine and its many victories, the English people began to think they had no choice but to throw in the towel. Realizing that the morale of his battle-fatigued country hung by a thread, Churchill gave one of the most inspiring speeches of all time—and his simple words quite possibly changed the course of the war: "Never, never, never give up." A wise wartime leader, Churchill made clear that "courage is the first of human qualities because it is the quality which guarantees all others."

But where does one get the courage, "the guts," to keep doing the hard things and not give up?

My Olympic coach, Eddie Reese, says that there are three things that make a great athlete. First, there's *genetics*. Being naturally tall, short, strong, flexible, light, dense—or whatever your defining characteristic is—gives you an advantage for certain sports and not for others. Eddie often says, "You don't pick the sport; the sport picks you."

The second factor is *work ethic*. This is all about your ability to focus the mind, to become a student of your sport, and to work your body harder and smarter than anyone else.

Third, and finally, there's what Coach Reese calls *the X-factor*. This is a little harder to objectify and describe. The athletes who have the X-factor thrive under pressure and get the job done, regardless of the odds. They are gamers—they know how to turn it on when it counts. And it's not so much that these athletes like winning, it's that they hate losing!

Dan Gable, the amazing wrestler, says something similar: "The first period is won by the best technician. The second period is won by the kid in the best shape. The third period is won by the kid with the biggest heart."[1] There's not much a person can do about genetics, but I believe that everyone can develop the "heart" of a champion.

Guts is a combination of all these things: courage, work ethic and heart—the X-factor. In this section, our athletes will share how they found the courage and motivation to work harder than others, the power to persevere through the pain barriers, and the perspective to thrive under pressure. Learning from them, you can too!

Note

1. Dan Gable, cited in David J. McGillivray, *The Last Pick: The Boston Marathon Race Director's Road to Success* (Emmaus, PA: Rodale Books, 2006).

The New Anger Management

Peter Westbrook
U.S. Olympic Bronze Medalist in Fencing

Anger is a killing thing: it kills the man who angers.
LOUIS L'AMOUR

If it hadn't been for my mom's bribe, chances are I would have met the same fate as many of the other kids in the projects of Newark—addicted to drugs, in jail or dead. My alcoholic dad had abandoned us when I was only three. As a Japanese immigrant and single parent, my mother struggled to keep food on the table. She sacrificed, sometimes working three jobs, to send me to parochial school.

Knowing I needed a positive environment, mom begged me to take fencing classes. She didn't know if I would be any good, but she remembered that fencing was an aristocratic sport in Japan and could be my ticket out of the projects. Already a gifted con artist, I told her that I would attend if she paid me $5.

Accepting her bribe, I started my first class at age 14. Actually, I enjoyed fencing and the encouragement I received, but I told my mom I didn't like it and wasn't going back. I managed to get another $5 out of her, but by then I was hooked. My fighting skills from the streets made me a natural, despite being a Japanese/African-American man in a white man's sport.

Harnessing my anger into sports, I excelled. But my anger haunted me later because I couldn't turn it off outside the fencing arena. Every little thing set off an almost uncontrollable rage. If a guy accidentally stepped on my toe in the subway, I'd cuss him out—I literally wanted to kill him.

Still, I managed to keep my anger under control—just barely—and focus on fencing. I won the New Jersey High School State Championship, earning a fencing scholarship to NYU. In college, I didn't believe there was a God, given all the violence and crime I had experienced. Though I wasn't walking with the Lord, He still ministered to me through the psychology courses I took, which addressed my rage by allowing me to revisit the violence and verbal abuse that had marked my childhood.

After college, I became a successful business salesman, leader and sports star. But the more I achieved in the world, the more depressed I became. In 1984, that emptiness led me on a journey to seek God—a journey that led me to win the bronze medal in fencing at the Los Angeles Games. My relationship with God led me to a higher level of athletic performance and fulfillment.

As I grew spiritually, my motivation for fencing gradually was transformed from anger and fear to love and gratitude. In the later years of my career, I fenced to serve and praise God.

In February 1991, I finally realized that God had blessed me and healed my anger for a purpose, not just so that other people would pat me on the back. This revelation inspired me to step out in faith and launch The Peter Westbrook Foundation, with the initial goal of helping save 20 kids from the projects of Newark. Since then, it's been one of my greatest joys to help thousands of inner-city children, some with more emotional baggage than you can imagine, learn to channel their anger in a positive direction and develop character through the sport of fencing.

Does anger control your life? Or are you motivated by love and gratitude toward God?

Get rid of all bitterness . . . along with every form of malice.
EPHESIANS 4:31

2

Overcoming Fear

Laura Wilkinson
U.S. Olympic Gold Medalist in Diving

Courage is fear that has said its prayers.
DOROTHY BERNARD

Everyone has fears. Sometimes fear can start from a thought or a challenge that really doesn't seem too bad at first. But if you don't overcome fear, it starts to grow. You can push fear away from your mind and try to forget it, but you always know it's there, lurking in the back of your mind.

After the 1998 World Championships, I experimented with a new dive, a back three-and-one-half somersault tuck. It didn't seem like a big deal, because I had learned several difficult dives before, but with several big meets coming up, we decided to wait and go with the dives I had already mastered. That summer, I grew very fearful of all my backward spinning dives after I became disoriented in a backward spinning arm-stand dive. Now, trying that new dive was the farthest thing from my wish list.

Between the 2000 Olympics, healing from foot surgery, graduating from college, and moving, I postponed the new dive numerous times. Before I knew it, almost five years had passed. Disappointed, I realized that fear was blocking me from trying. My mind had begun telling me that the dive was too difficult. I had built up such a momentous block of fear that I couldn't see beyond it.

Now, you're probably saying to yourself, *I know what you mean, but how do you make it go away?*

My answer is, you don't. Your problems aren't going to magically disappear and just go away. I ran out of ways to avoid my fear. I had to face it—not just the dive, but my thoughts about the dive.

So one day, I let myself contemplate the dive. I thought about everything that I could possibly be afraid of—smacking the board, getting the wind knocked out of me and becoming disoriented three stories in the air while dropping at 35 mph. My heart raced at these thoughts. But this time, I didn't push those frightening feelings away. Calming down, I realized that I had the tools to overcome that fear.

Saturday would be the day! The night before, I prayed intently. I asked God to calm my heart and give me confidence, to make my faith strong in Him so that I wouldn't fear or worry. Saturday morning before practice I was ready, physically and mentally. I read Scriptures that gave me peace before the Olympic trials—verses like 1 Corinthians 15:10, Isaiah 41:10,13 and Luke 17:6. Then my coach, Kenny Armstrong, spotted me in a belt over the trampoline so that I could feel the dive.

I was ready to go. When I went up to the 10-meter board, not only wasn't I scared, but I was also actually excited! I knew everything was going to be okay. And sure enough, the dive went just fine. Although I was a bit nervous during practice, I felt like a huge weight had been lifted off my shoulders.

Looking back, I am so thankful for the fear, because without it, I would never have known this wonderful feeling of overcoming!

Is fear holding you back in any area of your life from being all that God created you to be? If so, let go and let God. Exchange your fears for His supernatural peace.

Do not be anxious about anything.
PHILIPPIANS 4:6

3

Swimming Against
the Current

Jeremy Knowles
Bahamian Olympic Swim Team

*When we navigate through troubled waters, God is the Master of
not only the waves, but also the ship.*
DR. DAVID JEREMIAH

They said it couldn't be done! Only a few relay teams had successfully completed the ocean swim from Beacon's Cay, Exuma, to Nassau. Even in the comfort of a motorboat, it's a three-hour ride.
Could one swimmer endure the entire treacherous 30-mile swim?

October 1997, after months of preparation charting ocean currents and logistics, I set off from Beacon's Point at 7:17 A.M. following a yacht. Two other boats accompanied me, one on each side. A
9-person relay team rotated swimming 15-minute legs with me.

Sharks were definitely a concern swimming in the open ocean
in water that was 30-feet deep. Fortunately, I only encountered a
few nurse sharks and some friendly dolphins. The relay team paused
to play with the dolphins; however, knowing the swim would con-
sume every ounce of my energy, I had to press on.

Because of the intensity of the swim, my support team fed me
power bars, gels or grapes every 15 minutes to refuel my energy.
Exhausted, I focused on Philippians 4:13, remembering that I could
continue swimming because Christ strengthened me. Studying the
text earlier, I had realized that it was a humbling verse, coming from

a position of weakness rather than strength. I knew I had to rely on God alone, given the variables of weather, timing and current changes.

Strong currents made the grueling swim hours longer than I anticipated. My dependence on God intensified as nightfall came. I never planned on swimming in the ocean at night, unable to see beyond the lights of the boats. After sunset, I shivered in the cold water. We considered quitting and trying again when conditions improved. Instead, I put on a swimming cap and drank an occasional cup of hot chocolate in an effort to warm up.

I couldn't see the shoreline, but as the media reported my progress, people started parking their cars on the beach and turning on their headlights to guide my crew. At 10:17 P.M., 15 long hours after I started, I crawled ashore. Onlookers couldn't believe it! At only age 16, I had conquered the impossible, even in the dark. As word spread, several thousand people arrived to congratulate me. TV crews and local news stations covered the story. It's funny how I'm still more of a local hero for my ocean swim than for being an Olympian.

The perseverance I learned by swimming against the ocean current prepared me for the challenges to come, especially in college. Most of the other guys on my swim team didn't share my spiritual priorities. I feared rejection and had to learn how to hold fast to my faith and values in spite of peer pressure. It was a challenge knowing where to draw the line between being a loyal team member and a faithful follower of Christ. Yet many blessings sprang from my willingness to persevere, the greatest of which was watching three of my roommates make personal decisions for Christ as a result of my genuine witness.

Are you facing a challenge that requires you to swim against the current? It's not easy, but I encourage you to wait on the Lord. He has a plan for you and will give you the power to accomplish it.

But those who hope in the LORD will renew their strength.
ISAIAH 40:31

4

Divine Control

Jenny Johnson Jordan
U.S. Olympic Beach Volleyball Team

Knowing that I am not the one in control gives great encouragement.
Knowing the One who is in control is everything.
ALEXANDER MICHAEL

Honestly, I struggle with "control issues." Of course, we all have the need to control in some way or another. The truth is, however, that none of us can control all the circumstances of life—and if we think we have, we're simply fooling ourselves.

As athletes, we spend our lives trying to reassure ourselves that we are self-made people. We attribute the success we enjoy to our own preparation and hard work. Yet the Bible reminds us that God alone is in control of all things. The less we try to control, the more we can allow God to take over. It's a lesson I learned the hard way!

At the start of my 2007 Association of Volleyball Professionals (AVP) season, things looked promising for me and my partner. The previous year, we consistently finished in the top three at every tournament, and as the season came to a close, we enjoyed a No. 2 overall ranking. The top spot was within our reach as the 2007 season opened.

We quickly realized that our best-laid plans for success were far different from the crash that would soon ensue. Lower-ranked teams started to beat us! People started to ask, "What's wrong?

Are you injured? Will you guys break up?" It just didn't make any sense. We prepared for the season like we did every other. In fact, I felt we had even made some improvements in the off-season.

However, we continued to slip in the rankings. Extremely frustrated, my first instinct was to train more, spend more time at the beach, watch more game films and eat better. I thought to myself, *If I can just take control here, everything will work itself out.*

But as I began to look to God in prayer day after day, I felt God asking me to just be still. He kept reassuring me that He was in control and I didn't need to do anything. It was a difficult time in my career because I felt weak and out of control—letting go didn't come easily. But I found comfort in reading 2 Corinthians 12:9-10: "My grace is sufficient for you, for my power is made perfect in weakness. Therefore I will boast all the more gladly about my weaknesses, so that Christ's power may rest on me. That is why, for Christ's sake, I delight in weaknesses . . . For when I am weak, then I am strong."

In life, we always hear that control combined with strength is the recipe for success, but God sees things differently. The less control I have, the weaker I feel, which leads me to a total dependence on Christ—the place I need to be. It's not easy, but when I am there, God can really teach me about who He is and mold me into the kind of person He wants me to be.

How do you feel when you are out of control? Can you trust God to make His power perfect in your weakness?

For the foolishness of God is wiser than man's wisdom, and the weakness of God is stronger than man's strength.
1 CORINTHIANS 1:25

5

Feeling the Cold of Rejection

Vonetta Flowers
U.S. Olympic Gold Medalist in Bobsledding

When the heart weeps for what it has lost,
the spirit laughs for what it has found.
SUFI APHORISM

It is not easy to smile and stand on God's promises when it seems like God has let you down and your prayers have gone unanswered.

When I was nine years old, my track coach told me I had the potential to become the next Jackie Joyner Kersee. I dreamed of running in the Summer Olympics. Discouraged by the loss of my college coach and from suffering knee and ankle surgeries, I failed to qualify for the Summer Olympics in both 1996 and 2000.

Hanging up the spikes after 17 years of training was difficult, especially because I had not fulfilled my dream of competing in the Games. But I looked forward to becoming a mom and experiencing "normal" life as a newlywed without the pressure of training.

Then, suddenly, thanks to the crazy idea of my husband, Johnny, I found myself an unlikely member of the U.S. Bobsled Team. The first year in my new sport, as a Southerner who rarely ever saw snow, my partner and I found ourselves ranked No. 2 in the U.S. and No. 3 in the world. Even more ironically, I was headed to the 2002 Winter Olympics.

In most sports, if you're the best athlete on the team, there's typically no reason to believe that you'll get cut. But as soon as I became comfortable with our team's success and thought that my spot was secure, my hopes of becoming an Olympian were shattered again. I was shocked by my partner's decision to cut me from her team less than three months before the Olympic trials. To add insult to injury, I was replaced by an athlete formerly banned from track and field for using steroids.

I found myself asking why this had happened when it seemed like I was so close to fulfilling my dreams.

I returned home to Birmingham, Alabama, feeling helplessly rejected. Back at work as an assistant track coach, I tried not to think about the Winter Olympics. But I kept asking myself what I could have done differently to avoid being left out in the cold.

After being home for two weeks feeling sorry for myself, my husband encouraged me to start training again. I thought he was crazy! He said that God had put me in bobsled for a reason. He felt confident one of the other two U.S. drivers would eventually call and offer me an opportunity to compete for a spot on their team. Reluctantly, I agreed. As I questioned my direction and purpose, I found strength remembering that God had always delivered on His promises in the past, even when it seemed like the odds were against me.

After three weeks of training, my faith was strengthened. Both drivers called and invited me to join their teams. I accepted Jill Bakken's invitation—leading to my gold medal. Just when I thought it couldn't get any better, Jill and I were chosen to carry the Olympic flag in the closing ceremonies. It was one of the most humbling events in my life.

If you're facing the bitter sting of rejection, ask yourself if you are doing what God wants you to do. If so, continue to trust in God through the good and bad times until your breakthrough comes.

With man this is impossible, but with God all things are possible.
Matthew 19:26

6

Where Does My Help Come From?

Josh Davis
Three-time U.S. Olympic Gold Medalist in Swimming

Some forks in the road present us with greater consequences
than others. And at each juncture, with every divergence,
we can continue to move away from the life God intended for
us or we can maneuver back toward it.
JAMES EMERY WHITE

A few months before the 1996 Olympic trials, I received a package in the mail containing a collection of "good luck" chain letters designed to supposedly increase my chances of making the Centennial Olympics Team. Many of my national teammates who were also hoping to make the Games had already contributed and kept the chain going. Our captain urged us to pass the letters on to the rest of the team so that we wouldn't forfeit the good karma.

As I held the letters in my hand, several thoughts crossed my mind. I thought, *It's nice that my teammates want to help me fulfill my dream of making the team. And of course it would be nice to have a little extra help or good karma to make the Olympics . . . passing the chain letter on couldn't hurt. After all, if I did make the team, I might finally be able to afford to move out of our barebones, 600-square-foot apartment. Who knows, I might even find housing that had the luxury of central air and heat. And it would be great to be able to provide a decent life for my bride.*

But then I remembered that when I became a Christian, I gave God control of my life. Although it was a huge step of faith to get married in college and then to commit to train full time, God had always faithfully provided. It was odd, but I was actually content with our tiny garage apartment. Reflecting on God's past provision for our needs gave me the courage to trust Him with the results of the Olympic trials.

So I grabbed the package, took it outside and put a match to it. While the chain letters burned, I proclaimed, "God is my Provider, my Everything! My future is in His hands and He will never let me down. He's God and I'm not. If I need peace, God will provide it. If I need power, God will supply it. If I need favor, He will grant it when I need it and probably not a moment too soon!" As my Chaplain Dr. Null reminds me, "God is never late, but He's seldom early!" I knew I would be just fine without a chain letter, a rabbit's foot or even my lucky suit.

It felt so freeing burning those letters and releasing myself into God's hands instead of depending on something so inferior. Rather than the crutch of karma, I had the strength of the Cross. No good-luck charms or superstitious rituals can come close to the peace, power and presence of our King Jesus!

Who or what do you look to for peace and power? What do you lean on when things are uncertain? Who holds your future in their hands? Ask God to free you from anything that is standing in the way of your becoming all He created you to be.

I lift up my eyes to the hills—where does my help come from?
My help comes from the LORD, the Maker of heaven and earth.
PSALM 121:1-2

7

Pursuing God

Ugur Taner
Turkish Olympic Swim Team

He who sends the storm steers the vessel.
THOMAS ADAMS

I started swimming as a 10-year-old. By the time I was 14, I had set four National Age Group Records. I went on to swim for 17 years, but only in my last year did I swim for Christ.

Prior to that final year, I experienced a deep valley. I even questioned whether I wanted to continue swimming. I was on the U.S. National Swim Team, and "going for the gold" was supposed to be a big deal, but racing just didn't seem to make sense anymore. So I asked myself, *What else besides swimming am I going to pursue with that same intensity in my life?* I started realizing that it was no longer going to be a gold medal.

What—or who—did I decide to pursue? The Lord. In January 2000, I accepted Christ! With this decision, I developed a fresh perspective on my final year as a professional swimmer. My training improved, and I felt more confident every week in the water. With two months to go, I was swimming close to my top times for midseason. Performing at my best, I was at peace, knowing that the outcome was in His hands.

After representing Turkey in the 1992 Olympics, my desire leading into 2000 was to return and represent the United States. However, the U.S. Olympic trials for swimming is the fastest, most competitive swim meet in the world. Less than 1 percent of all swimmers at the trials actually make the team, so you can imagine the level of stress I felt preparing for competition.

After swimming well in the qualifying rounds, I was seeded in fifth place going into the finals. Because they take six spots in the 200-meter freestyle, I was hopeful that I would make my second Olympics—my first as part of the U.S. team. I swam just four-tenths of a second off my lifetime best with a time of 1:49:00, but the sixth-place finisher swam a 1:48:99. I was the seventh-place finisher and missed making the Olympics by 1/100th of a second!

Needless to say, falling short of my dream by the smallest of margins was disheartening. However, I had another one of my favorite races later in the evening—the 200-meter butterfly. Leading into the trials, I was one of the best swimmers in this particular event, so I was, once again, hopeful to make the team. I did my best, but it was not enough. I missed my last chance at making the team. With that, my swimming career ended.

I cried. The next 24 hours were difficult in many ways as I faced the death of my dreams. But the very next morning, I sat in a swimmer's chapel led by my best friend, Josh Davis. Sharing my experience, I reflected on the fact that God still loved me. Even though I had no idea what God was doing in my life, I trusted in His providence.

When I look back on that experience, I see that I walked through that valley with peace. If I had gone through that loss on my own, without God's help, I'm sure I wouldn't be where I am today. My wife, Liesl, and three kids, Brooks, Channing and Vaughn, can all attest to that!

Are you pursuing your relationship with God with more intensity than any other area in your life? Remember, God's peace is beyond anything this world can offer.

In his heart a man plans his course, but the LORD determines his steps.
PROVERBS 16:9

8

Training Worship

Penny Heyns
South-African Olympic Gold Medalist in Swimming

*Anything you can do can become an act of worship. . . . Nothing
makes God happier than people praising Him through the activities
He has gifted them to do.*
CAT REDDICK, U.S. OLYMPIC SOCCER GOLD MEDALIST

We often think worship is restricted to singing songs at church on
Sunday mornings. The swimming pool was God's classroom for
teaching me that true worship is a daily attitude of the heart. It's
acknowledging God's worthiness to be the One we give our all to.

After the Atlanta Olympics in 1996, when I became the first
woman swimmer ever to win a gold medal in both the 100- and
200-meter breaststroke, I fell into a two-year slump. By May 1998, I
found myself struggling to continue swimming. After much prayer
and soul searching—even considering retirement—I relocated from
Nebraska to Calgary, Canada, to continue training. Thinking my
days of being the fastest swimmer were probably over, my primary
objective was to be a godly witness to my new teammates.

But the first day of training, my coach instructed me to swim
at the far end of the pool and do 6 sets of 800s. This meant swimming up and down a black line on my own for over 80 minutes. My
heart sank. I wondered, *How does God plan to use me if I can't even
speak to my fellow athletes?* Swimming in isolation, I found myself
grumbling and complaining.

Later that evening, reading 1 Thessalonians 5:16-18 ("Be joyful always; pray continually; give thanks in all circumstances, for this is God's will for you in Christ Jesus"), I realized that I hadn't been swimming with a thankful heart. Suddenly, it dawned on me that God wanted me to worship Him as I trained. I sensed God was saying to me, "Penny, as you swim up and down this black line, this is your opportunity to worship Me. Every single breaststroke kick and pull that you do is the same as raising your hands in church and praising Me. I'll teach you to worship Me through your talent."

Swimming wasn't just about the medals or recognition or doing a specific training set for my coach or myself anymore. Instead, I committed to giving my whole being and heart to God in every moment of my swimming. As I began focusing on God in the water every day, worship became a habit. Soon, regardless of how I felt, I looked forward to going to the pool in the afternoons to worship my Lord.

A year later, in mid-June 1999, I competed at a swim meet in Los Angeles. Coming off one of the heaviest training cycles of my career, I felt drained and completely dependent on God.

The first race, the 200-meter breaststroke, wasn't my favorite event. As I stepped onto the starting block, I silently prayed, "Lord, as I swim up and down in this race, I'm going to focus on You. Every single kick and pull cycle is going to be my act of worship. I trust Your will for my life."

The first three lengths were smooth, well paced and relaxed. As I turned for the fourth and last length, I kicked off the wall, singing in my heart, "My strength is in You, Lord; my hope is in You, Lord." As I worshiped Him, each stroke felt stronger. When I touched the wall, much to my surprise, I learned I had just set a new world record!

Concentrating on God as I raced, I broke three more world records that meet, including my own 1996 world record in the

100-meter breaststroke. And that was just the beginning. Within three months, God helped me set a total of 11 world records.

But world records, in themselves, aren't that important to God—He's more interested in the process and what we learn on the journey. As I look back on my swimming career, it's not the world records that thrill me most. My greatest joy is knowing that God used my love of swimming to draw me closer to Him.

I challenge you to live a life seeking to worship God every single moment in all you do. Whether you're training or competing, resting or enjoying time with friends or family, honor God. During good times and in difficult times, praise Him. Preparing for the biggest event of your life or during your everyday routine, celebrate His presence.

And whatever you do, whether in word or deed, do it all in the name of the Lord Jesus, giving thanks to God the Father through him.
Colossians 3:17

Worship the Lord with gladness; come before him with joyful songs.
Psalm 100:2

Never be lazy in your work, but serve the Lord enthusiastically.
Romans 12:11, *TLB*

Preparation of Praise

Jennifer Barringer
U.S. Track and Field Team

One thing worship costs us is our self-centeredness.
You cannot exalt God and yourself at the same time.
RICK WARREN

There was a point in my racing career when I felt as if each race coming up was the most important in my life. A healthy hunger for success had turned into a starvation for achievement. The pressure of performing better each time was overwhelming.

So I turned to God. I asked for wisdom to guide my lifestyle habits in a way that would lead me to success. I prayed for perseverance to get through the long workouts and the countless miles of training. I pleaded for the strength to not only get through the next race, but also to make it the best I had raced in my life. I asked and asked. I prayed and prayed. I thought I knew what I needed.

I got to the starting line of the last race of my season. Months upon months of training had brought me to this place. The gun went off, and I ran strong and confident—until tragedy hit. Less than two laps in, one of my opponents clipped my shoe. In one instant, I went from a strong favorite to the biggest underdog. I tugged violently at my shoe as I watched the pack of women, along with my whole season, run off around the turn without me.

In the following weeks, my coach and I decided to extend my season so that it wouldn't have to end with such an upsetting event. The miles were even harder when I thought about how I had failed to reach my expectations. The movie of those women running away kept replaying in my mind as I trained.

And so I turned to God again, but this time in a spirit of praise. I thanked God for creating me to run. I praised Him for all of the experiences my sport had given me. I praised Him for challenging me to fight for what I had worked so hard for.

Two weeks later, I toed the line against the same women I had faced in the previous race, along with the defending national champion in my event. I knew there would be no room for errors. Yet in that moment, my heart praised God for this opportunity. I was ready to enter battle with the Lord ahead of me. I went on to claim a dramatic victory by a very small margin and set a new record.

As soon as I finished, a reporter asked me how good redemption felt. It was at that moment that I realized how much my heart had grown and changed over the previous two weeks. I had never thought of extending my season for revenge or redemption. I had been able to put the pain of the previous upset behind me and run this race for what it was.

God wants us to succeed. He wants us to be excellent. I was asking for all of the right guidance, but I had lost sight of why I was racing in the first place. When I humbled myself to praise Him, I found confidence to succeed without earthly pride. I put God first, acknowledging His control.

Are you allowing God to go ahead of you in battle? When God goes first, you can let Him take control and allow praise to fill your heart.

Enter his gates with thanksgiving and his courts with praise;
give thanks to him and praise his name.
PSALM 100:4

1 0

Learning from Others

Mark Knowles
Four-time Bahamian Olympian in Tennis

Attitude is a little thing that makes a big difference.
WINSTON CHURCHILL

One minute my younger brother, Byron, was a healthy, happy nine-year-old boy. The next minute he collapsed and was seconds away from death, requiring an emergency airlift from the Bahamas to Miami. I was 16 and felt so helpless and out of control. But I grew up in a Christian home, and my family leaned on God together. After successful brain surgery, my brother eventually made a full recovery. That was my first memorable experience with faith and with God being in control.

My brother's mysterious illness brought an awareness to me at an early age that we're not in control of life as much as we want to be. I didn't take life for granted anymore. I learned that while I can't always control my circumstances, I can always choose my attitude. This lesson has served me well in tennis doubles.

Another valuable lesson I've learned is that the more I focus on me (not in a selfish way, but on improving myself), the more valuable I become to my partner. It's easy to want to change something you don't like in your partner instead of working to better yourself (this is true in marriage as well).

My tennis partner, Daniel, and I had the longest running doubles partnership on the Pro Tour—10 years. We share the same birthday and are only a year apart in age. We served as groomsmen for each other's weddings. Our families were intertwined.

Then in May 2007, midway through the season, he announced that he wanted a new partner. I was so disappointed and hurt. But instead of sulking, I kept practicing hard. Three weeks later, in the midst of this shakeup, we won the French Open together. He agreed to remain teammates through the 2007 U.S. Open, where we finished in the semifinals.

I thought we could achieve more as a team—even finally capture Wimbledon and join eight other teams in tennis history who have won the Grand Slam—but Daniel had other plans. The media tried to get me to verbally trash my partner for bailing on me when we had finished the season ranked No. 2 in the world. But my biblical foundation had taught me the principle of not speaking evil of a friend (this is especially invaluable in a marriage—never talk trash about your partner, even if you split up).

Take the opportunity to learn from your partner. I'm more boisterous; Daniel helped me become more level. And I helped him escape his introverted shell. Although Daniel and I had a fantastic ride together for 10 years, I've learned to trust God's control and have moved on. When He closes one door, another one opens. I can't control another person, but I can always follow my motto: Do my best and give 100 percent!

If you're in a partnership (whether it's in sports, business or marriage), are you focused on improving yourself? Or are you trying to change your partner's weaknesses? Are you undercutting your relationship by talking badly about your partner? Or are you taking the opportunity to learn from his or her strengths?

Why not make a personal commitment today to focus on doing your best and giving 100 percent? Then leave the rest up to God.

Don't criticize and speak evil about each other, dear brothers.
JAMES 4:11, *TLB*

11

What Happened?

Madeline Manning Mims
U.S. Olympic Gold Medalist in Track

God marks across some of our days, "Will explain later."
VANCE HAVNER

When God calls me to an assignment, it always seems to be public and sometimes embarrassing. It's like I am on display for the world to see my strengths and weaknesses.

In 1976, after setting a new world record in the 3,000-meter run at a little side meet, I was favored to win the women's 800-meter in Montreal at the Summer Olympics. But something went very wrong.

In my semifinal race, the unthinkable happened: I ran a very lethargic race and couldn't break out of myself, no matter how hard I tried. My body just refused to obey instructions. I seemed to be stuck on slow-motion auto-pilot. Confused, stunned, fearful and in disbelief, I walked off the track—last.

News media appeared from everywhere, asking, "What happened?" If I only had an answer that made sense to me, I could have told them, but I didn't really know. I just couldn't make my body go.

A teammate came over and comforted me, but I was too paralyzed to even cry. After an amazing comeback, setting the world record, I crashed without warning. No injuries, no illnesses, no mental breakdown, no excuses to explain what had happened. *All that work over the years . . . for what?* I wondered. I felt embarrassed and downright shamed.

Leaving the Games depressed, I received an invitation to run one more time in a U.S. versus U.S.S.R. meet in Maryland before returning home. I only said yes because they offered to give me a stipend big enough to cover my rent when I got home. Because the Games were over, no one—especially not me—felt like running.

I approached the line not caring about the outcome, until a friend and teammate of mine hollered out words of encouragement to me from the stands. It was like being reminded of the purpose for which I had been born: "Run for Jesus!"

I felt adrenaline pumping through my body as it prepared to run its normal elite level. I prayed a quick prayer, "Okay, Father, this one's for You. It's my tribute run to Jesus." My nerves shot off like Fourth of July fireworks as I stepped to the line, fired up to run the race of my life.

I finished simultaneously with a Russian runner—our finish was a personal best for both of us and a new American record for me (1:57:87—even today, this is still considered a tough time to beat at the world-class level). I also became friends with the Russian runner. By honoring God in the presence of witnesses, my tribute run, surprisingly, worked out to my good.

Even when we don't understand what God is doing in the moment, He always knows what He is achieving for the long run. He's more interested in our character than our comfort.

Think about how trustworthy our Father is. Then ask yourself, *Will I trust in His Sovereignty when I face questionable or humbling circumstances?* I hope the answer is yes!

And we know that all things work together for good to them that love God, to them who are the called according to His purpose.
ROMANS 8:28, *KJV*

12

Moving On from Failure

Matt Scoggin
U.S. Olympic Diving Team

*The most common trait I have found in all
successful people is that they have conquered the
temptation to give up.*

PETER LOWE

It's never easy to fail. But no one wants to fail in front of a global audience. After years of preparation for the 1992 Barcelona Olympics, I was in the running for a 10-meter diving medal. Then the unthinkable happened.

As I launched my dive, my left hand slipped, sending me into an uncontrolled spin at over 35 miles per hour. I couldn't get into the tuck position. Completely lost in the backward somersaults, I smacked flat on my back on the water's surface. It was as if everyone watching around the world had the same simultaneous reaction: "Ouch! That must have hurt!" Medical personnel rushed in to make sure I wasn't seriously injured.

There were rumors that I punctured a kidney. Although it looked much worse, the physical sting of the failed dive was over in less than a minute. It was the sting of embarrassment that lingered a little longer thanks to continuous instant replays throughout the Games, accompanied by the two commentators: "Oh, no!" and then, "An absolute failed dive for Matt Scoggin!"

But the competition wasn't over yet. After my infamous historic back flop, I climbed back up the platform, knowing that I had to shake my failure and move on. I'll never forget my next dive. When they announced my name, the entire stadium of over 10,000 people stood to their feet and gave me the heartiest, most heartwarming standing ovation you could ever imagine. Even now, I can't begin to express how amazing it felt to know the crowd was really behind me. Receiving their compassionate ovation almost moved me to tears. I guess everyone loves an underdog who doesn't give up. In the end, with several more good dives, I was able to pull back up to tenth place.

Making the "bloopers and blunders" highlight reel of the Barcelona Olympics definitely wasn't what I had in mind. But looking back, I know that God providentially used that awful back flop for a purpose. Today as the head coach of the University of Texas Diving Team, I train some of the best divers in the country. When they fall short of their lofty goals, I have instant credibility when I encourage them that it's not the end of the world. I'm living proof that you can get back up and successfully try again.

Mistakes happen even to the best-trained people—Babe Ruth struck out more times than he hit homeruns. But failure can also be instigated by inexperience, character flaws, laziness or sin. In the Bible, King David made a colossal blunder in his indiscretion with Bathsheba. But when he repented, God still called David a man after His own heart. God is a God of second chances.

Do you remember a time when you were humiliated by failure? Is failure a stone that crushes and paralyzes you, or does it become a stepping-stone that leads you to the next level? While it's great to learn from failure, focusing on it will only hold you back from achieving the greatness God has in store for you.

For though a righteous man falls seven times, he rises again.
PROVERBS 24:16

Expressing Disappointment

Jenny Johnson Jordan
U.S. Olympic Beach Volleyball Team

The greatness comes not when things go always good for you.
But the greatness comes when you're really tested, when you take some
knocks, some disappointments, when sadness comes.
RICHARD M. NIXON

I am a passionate person: I tend to cry easily at movies and during emotional commercials. I'm no different on the volleyball court. I am the vocal leader of my team, pumping my fists and leaving bruises due to overzealous high-fives. Great plays excite me! I've been known to jump around the court unabashedly after a big win. But what happens when I lose?

At the 2000 Olympic Games in Sydney, my teammate, Annett Davis, and I were favored to win a medal for the United States in women's beach volleyball. Some experts had even picked us to win the gold. Personally, I expected big things as well. Unfortunately, however, we finished a disappointing fifth place.

Although shocked by the outcome, I tried to keep a brave face. Following the match, I felt numb as I gave stock answers in our interviews. It wasn't until after I left the press conference and saw my family that I finally felt the freedom to release my emotions. I hugged my brother; I couldn't let go of him. Standing in the middle of a crowd, I cried uncontrollably. After two hard years of traveling, competing, training and making countless sacrifices, my chances of winning a medal at these Olympics were over. I was visibly crushed. Later, I sat in the stands watching the last match of the day, still in disbelief that I was out of the competition.

I used to believe that "good, believing" Christians shouldn't show their disappointment. I often wore my "game face" to mask my emotions when something was wrong so that no one would question my trust in God. Sometimes, as Christians, we hide behind these masks because we don't want people to see the real us—the hurting, struggling or even sad us. We even try to hide from ourselves and from God. My defeat at the Games taught me that expressing disappointment doesn't mean I trust God any less. On the contrary, being honest about my disappointment draws me closer to God.

The Bible gives us many examples of men and women who trusted God but still expressed real emotions of anguish and pain. Hannah was unable to conceive a child and, as a result, she wept and did not eat. When Job experienced the ultimate tragedy—losing his family—he was transparent with his feelings without ever losing his faith. And one does not have to look very far into the book of Psalms to find genuine cries of distress and deliverance.

As an athlete, a wife, a mother and a friend, I strive every day to express myself authentically, the way God intended. Although I may experience disappointments in this life, I can be honest with my emotions while trusting that God is in control and that His plans are the best for my life.

Are you tired of hiding your sadness? Are you ready to "get real" with the Lord? I pray that you will allow His love to free you to be authentic in your emotions as you live out the highs and lows of the Christian life.

There is a time for everything, and a season for every
activity under heaven.
ECCLESIASTES 3:1

14

The Secret Is . . .

Annett Davis
U.S. Olympic Beach Volleyball Team

*Obedience to God's will is the secret of spiritual knowledge
and insight. It is not willingness to know, but willingness
to do God's will that brings certainty.*
ERIC LIDDELL

Balancing my roles as a homeschool mom and a pastor's wife, on top of traveling internationally as a professional volleyball player, is often a bit challenging. I'm frequently asked, "What is your secret?"

In the rush of life, we're constantly searching for answers on how to make life easier. Everyone is curious to discover if the grass is truly greener somewhere else. Most people who ask me about "my secret" falsely assume that I'm a superwoman and that my life is picture perfect. They don't understand that I've lived through some painful experiences and that balancing my hectic schedule isn't as easy as it may look.

But my true "secret" really isn't a secret—it's easily found in the number-one bestselling book of all times. Its promises are truly 100-percent guaranteed. My key resource, God's inspired Word, has been guiding people for thousands of years. We just need to read it more. The truth about life, love, family, friendships, law, business, leadership—you name it—can all be found in God's Word.

And it's no secret that God wants each of us to live our lives in relationship with Him. He tells us in His Word how to live—nothing hidden, no decoding needed. The book of Deuteronomy 6:5 tells us, "Love the LORD your God with all your heart and with all your soul and with all your strength," which is the first step to living a great life.

There are so many promises that are in God's Word, promises given specifically for you and me. If you want to discover truth that transcends time and transforms lives, take time to read the Manufacturer's Handbook for Human Life—the Bible. You won't be disappointed. There isn't a topic it doesn't cover.

Reading Psalms and Proverbs is a great starting place. The book of Psalms gives encouragement for the up-and-down moments of life, while Proverbs provides divine wisdom for parenting, relationships and business.

Is the Bible your number-one resource for daily living? Why not take a problem you are facing today and spend a few moments looking for an answer from the Creator of the universe? God promises to give wisdom to those who ask.

All Scripture is God-breathed and is useful for teaching,
rebuking, correcting and training in righteousness.
2 TIMOTHY 3:16

As for God, his way is perfect; the word of the LORD is flawless.
He is a shield for all who take refuge in him.
2 SAMUEL 22:31

For everything that was written in the past was written to teach us,
so that through endurance and the encouragement of the
Scriptures we might have hope.
ROMANS 15:4

15

Conforming to Jesus

Brooke Abel
U.S. Olympic Synchronized Swimming

If a man does not keep pace with his companions, perhaps it is because he hears a different drummer . . .
THOREAU

If you don't stand for something, you will fall for everything.
REVEREND PETER MARSHALL, 1947 SENATE CHAPLAIN

In my sport, synchronized swimming, the goal is to conform to the group. We want to appear as one unit moving fluidly through the water.

At a Trophy Cup Meet in Russia, we did just that. We had only three weeks to choreograph a performance—which normally takes about three months—and we nailed it!

Though entering as underdogs, we claimed the victory and handed Russia its first defeat in more than 10 years. It was thrilling to see how we could come together and conform to the routine as a group and do something very special in such a short amount of time.

In the water, I conform to my team, but out of the water I try to conform to Jesus. Contrary to what I do in the pool, I resist the temptation to blend in with our culture, and I make strides to set myself apart in my words and deeds.

Have you compromised your beliefs to blend in? Are you conforming to something that is separating you from God? Allow God to draw you near and transform you into His image.

Do not conform any longer to the pattern of this world,
but be transformed by the renewing of your mind.
Then you will be able to test and approve what God's will is—
his good, pleasing and perfect will.
Romans 12:2

If anyone would come after me, he must deny himself
and take up his cross and follow me. For whoever wants
to save his life will lose it, but whoever loses his life for me
and for the gospel will save it.
Mark 8:34-35

No servant can serve two masters. Either he will hate
the one and love the other, or he will be devoted to the
one and despise the other.
Luke 16:13

16

Overcoming Temptation

David Robinson
San Antonio Spurs MVP
Three-time U.S. Olympic Basketball Medalist

*Living a pure and righteous life doesn't happen by accident.
It takes a decision to be purposeful and diligent about
our thoughts, words and actions.*

BRIENNE MURK

Many superstars and leaders fall because of temptation. I'm often asked how I was able to maintain my reputation while playing in the NBA.

As a young man, I always had a certain level of innocence with me that kept me from getting into a lot of trouble in the first place. When the opportunities were there, I was always wary of them. I would think, *That's not right.* My senior prom was the only real date I went on all throughout high school. Girls thought I was shy, but I was just inexperienced and didn't know how to date.

A lot of the temptation never even occurred to me. When I was at the Naval Academy, I saw others who frequently got away with breaking regulations. That wasn't even in my range of thinking. I'd scold, "Why are you doing that? That's against the rules. You could get into so much trouble!"

They would laugh at me in disbelief, "Come on, man. I can't believe you're worried about getting into trouble." I wasn't even a real Christian yet, but I avoided a lot of trouble because the consequences associated with it didn't appeal to me.

When I got to the NBA, I didn't go to clubs because I figured that wasn't going to be the place where I'd meet my future wife. There is some value to not exposing yourself to certain things; to say, *I'm not going to listen to this type of music, I'm not going to watch these types of movies on TV, and I'm not going to put myself in certain situations where I'm going to be tempted. I'm just a man like any other man, and if I see something, I'm going to want it.*

My rookie year in the NBA was one of self-discovery. I was suddenly surrounded by beautiful women and all of the things that money can buy you. I was always tempted to step out and try some of the experiences I had never been exposed to. This was the perfect setting for my faith to get stronger. I always knew what I should be doing, but I just needed Jesus to give me the example and the will to pursue holiness.

In 1991, I accepted Jesus as the Lord and Savior of my life. That's when I learned of the biblical principles of avoiding temptation. Then I married my wife, Valerie. Philippians 4:8 instructs us to keep our eyes on what is good and what is perfect and what is right and to keep our minds on those things so that we don't corrupt ourselves. Once you expose yourself to evil, you end up thinking about the wrong things all the time. And it's especially hard to resist temptation when it's all you can think about.

Now that I'm a believer, one of my key ways of dealing with temptation is to always have Scripture ready in my heart and in my mind. One verse that really inspires me is Job 31:1, where Job talks about making a covenant with his eyes not to look at a woman with lust. I write key verses on sticky notes and post them throughout my house and office. Three verses that are on my desk are:

- "Therefore be very courageous to keep and to do all that is written in the Book of the Law of Moses, lest you turn aside from it to the right hand or to the left. . . . but you shall hold fast to the LORD your God, as you have done to this day" (Joshua 23:6,8, *NKJV*).

- "Let your eyes look straight ahead, and your eyelids look right before you. Ponder the path of your feet, and let all your ways be established" (Proverbs 4:25-26, *NKJV*).

- "[T]hat you may become blameless and harmless, children of God without fault in the midst of a crooked and perverse generation, among whom you shine as lights in the world, holding fast the word of life" (Philippians 2:15-16, *NKJV*).

These are things that I have to hold on to if I start thinking wrong. It's like my rope that I grab on to. It helps me think through the consequences of sin. I correct my false thinking by digging into the Word of God.

A second key that I've discovered is to always have people in my mind that I can draw from for accountability. I have friends that I call when I face temptation. We're not called to do life on our own. Hebrews 12:1 tells us that we're surrounded by a great cloud of witnesses. It's critical to have someone to call when we need some perspective, if something we shouldn't watch pops up on the Internet or TV, we get a financial offer that is unethical, or a very attractive person that's not your spouse flirts with you.

Temptation will come. Be ready by writing some key verses on sticky notes and memorizing one each week. Make a list now of people you can call when you aren't thinking right and program their numbers into your cell phone. May you shine for Him today and always!

I have hidden your word in my heart that I might not sin against you.
PSALM 119:11

17

No More Compromising

Leah O'Brien-Amico
Three-time U.S. Olympic Softball Team Gold Medalist

*No Compromise is what the whole Gospel of Jesus is all about . . .
in a day when believers seem to be trying to please both the world
and the Lord . . . there is only one answer . . . Deny yourself,
take up your cross and follow Him!*

KEITH GREEN

Even before I invited God into my life as a collegiate softball player,
I didn't have as many vices as some athletes—and I only drank oc-
casionally at parties.

About a year and a half into my spiritual journey, I enjoyed my
Bible study, but I still had a lot to learn and apply. After casually
talking to one of my non-Christian friends about the celebration
for my twenty-second birthday the night before, she made a comment I'll never forget: "Look at you. Here you are going out and
drinking and wearing those cross earrings."

Although her words stung, hitting me like a ton of bricks, they
sparked a defining moment in my spiritual life. That birthday
marked my last alcoholic drink. It's ironic that God used a non-
Christian in my life to set me free and to challenge me to sell out
to Him. I decided, "God, I don't want to be a stumbling block for
others to come to You. I want to give it all to You. I trust You, and
I don't care what anyone else thinks."

People noticed a big difference in the way I lived after that.

Our peers often view Christianity as a bunch of rules that prevent us from enjoying life and having fun. But I found unbelievable freedom in totally selling out to God.

Have you decided to follow God in every area of your life, or are you compromising? Ask God to search your heart today.

Be careful, however, that the exercise of your freedom
does not become a stumbling block to the weak.
1 CORINTHIANS 8:9

Trust in the LORD with all your heart
and lean not on your own understanding.
PROVERBS 3:5

No servant can serve two masters. Either he will hate the
one and love the other, or he will be devoted to the one
and despise the other.
LUKE 14:33

18

Unanswered Prayers

Jennifer Barringer
U.S. Track and Field Team

*I'm trying to accept that sometimes my prayers are answered, "No."
Sometimes when the Lord doesn't give me something or answer my prayer
right away, He's protecting me. I may not be ready for a certain thing at
this point in my life. I just have to be patient and totally trust Him.*

MARY LOU RETTON

When I was a little girl, I remember my parents telling me that there was no such thing as an unanswered prayer. God answers all of our prayers in one of three ways: "Yes," "No" or "Not now." From there, we just have to trust that He's in control.

Even though I had this guidance from a young age, I still struggle with practical application. It's not easy when you don't get the answer you've been looking for, and it can be even harder when you just have to wait. But as I've grown into an adult and as a Christian, I have found that waiting on the Lord results in abundant blessings!

One winter, after relocating across the country and beginning my first year as a college athlete, I got a little too greedy and found myself sidelined with a femoral stress reaction. My passion had been ripped from my hands due to my own excessive drive. For two weeks, I battled through my first real winter (I grew up in Florida!) on crutches, with little knowledge of the actual cause of my pain. We waited on a bone scan to determine the final verdict. I was devastated and lost. I called on God for healing and restoration. I wanted Him to fix it! I just knew that when we got the results of the scan, they were going to be negative.

The bone scan came back positive. I had been so optimistic—when I found out I was in for at least four more weeks of crutches, I felt abandoned. Why had God allowed all of this to happen, and *then* not answered my prayers that I felt were full of a mountain's worth of faith?

Still, with the encouragement of friends and family, along with their own prayers, I picked my head up and got to work. I cross-trained like crazy, accepting my condition and working through it as well as I could.

The following spring was track season. I returned to the sport with a new energy, ready to take on the world. The break from running had really transformed me as a runner. The cross-training workouts were intense, but my mind was so desperate to get back on the roads. When I finally did, it was a tough comeback, but I was so ready for it!

That season I trained smarter under excellent coaching. My "unanswered prayer" turned into a spark that not only got me through my first collegiate track season but also led to a national championship as a freshman!

To this day, I thank God for taking control and not granting my plea. Racing through the winter and then into the spring would have worn me out for sure. That crucial rest and the renewed focus were essential to the tremendous success I experienced later on—and I wouldn't trade it for the world!

Next time you find yourself in a jam and God doesn't seem to be coming through for you, remember to trust in Him. When we put Him in control, He might just one-up our request and bless us with more than we ever imagined!

Trust in the LORD . . . and lean not on your own understanding.
PROVERBS 3:5

19

Lessons in True Joy

Amanda Borden
1996 Captain of the Gold Medal U.S. Gymnastics Team

It's never too late to change and begin experiencing the fullness of a life filled with joy and peace, a life built on the bedrock of confidence in God.

JIM GRAFF

Being robbed can be a joy buster. After eight years of training, I placed seventh at the 1992 U.S. Olympic trials and qualified for the team. My joy was short-lived, however, when a political decision robbed me of my spot. I couldn't believe it when they told me I was too young, that they were passing me over for another, more-experienced gymnast.

Though I was encouraged to keep practicing for the next Games, I knew there were no guarantees for a spot on the team, even if I earned it. What if I gave my all to training another four years and wasn't picked again? Practice just wasn't the same. I couldn't find joy anymore in my daily routine. Discouraged, I quit gymnastics.

Throughout my life, I've regularly prayed each night. During my prayer time, I kept sensing that God still had a plan for me in gymnastics and this setback had been a test. So my retirement only lasted three days!

During that time, my coach, Mary Lee Tracy, was a blessing. She prayed with me and another teammate before each competition. Her Monday night Bible study helped me reclaim my joy and taught me how real, relevant and exciting the Bible really is.

After recovering from multiple back injuries, I broke my hand just two months before the 1996 Olympic trials. Despite my injuries, I continued to trust God's plan. That peace freed me to work hard and to leave the results to Him. By His grace, I tried out, had fun and made the team. When I went to Atlanta just weeks later, I felt amazingly decisive, poised, prepared and ready to serve. My teammates elected me team captain. Although nervous, I decided, "Whatever happens, I'm going to have the best time of my life!"

Getting ready to march into the gymnastics stadium, I experienced a special God moment. I noticed one of my teammates lacked joy and looked overwhelmed. I encouraged her, "Dominique, we've done everything we can to prepare and it's in God's hands now. Let's just go have fun and enjoy this!"

We had the time of our lives, and we became the first gymnastics team in U.S. history to win the Olympic gold medal. Standing on the top podium with the rest of the "Magnificent Seven," I was overwhelmed with joy, reflecting on how much I love gymnastics and all of the people who helped me reach that moment.

In 2005, when Dominique was inducted into the Gymnastics Hall of Fame, it was so special when she recounted how much my encouragement in Atlanta had meant to her.

Today, I've started my own gymnastics school in Arizona. God teaches me something every day through the 650 kids I oversee with my other coaches. I'm constantly learning new things as a wife, business owner and new mom. But after all these years, the one thing God continues to remind me is that He's still in control and we can trust Him with the results.

Is somebody or something robbing you of your joy? Regardless of your circumstances, ask the Lord to make His joy your strength today!

I came that they may have life, and may have it abundantly.
JOHN 10:10, *NASB*

The Best Compliment Ever

John Naber
Four-time U.S. Olympic Gold Medalist in Swimming

*Perhaps you will forget tomorrow the kind words you say today,
but the recipient may cherish them over a lifetime.*
DALE CARNEGIE

Most athletes at the Games begin their career by studying a role
model in their sport. My hero, Roland Matthes, was the defending
Olympic champion in my favorite events, the backstrokes.

Roland, a devout Communist from East Germany, entered the
1974 swimming season undefeated in his best events since the 1968
Olympic Games. He seemed invincible, breaking his own world records almost at will. He spoke almost no English and never went out
of his way to make friends with swimmers from the West. He also
seemed to shy away from interviews.

In 1974, the East German National team visited California for
a dual meet against the U.S. swimmers. Most experts predicted the
East Germans would win every woman's event, and the American men would sweep every race except the backstrokes. Pressure
mounted as I realized America's chance to win the meet weighed
squarely on my ability to upset my champion.

Studying the video of the great German, I noticed that Roland
accelerated into each of the turns while most of his opponents
slowed down, fearing they might hit the wall. By "hitting the turns,"

Roland came off the wall a stroke ahead, and from his competitors' point of view, he disappeared from sight. His vanishing act devastated his opponents' confidence.

When I raced Roland in the finals of the dual meet, I concentrated on increasing my pace into the turns. Instead of extending his lead over me on the wall, Roland found himself falling behind. This shocked him—and helped me defeat him in all three of our head-to-head contests that meet. The Americans won the meet, but Roland's records remained intact.

Two years later, in the semifinal of the 100-meter backstroke at the 1976 Olympic Games, I won my heat and finally broke Roland's world record. Though Roland had qualified for the finals in an earlier heat, he was there, in the warm-down pool beneath the bleachers, to watch me best his record.

Entering the warm-down pool in an adjacent lane, I felt both proud of my accomplishment and guilty for removing my hero's name from the record books. Then Roland came sliding over the lane rope and "chucked" me under the chin with a playful fist. Smiling at me he said, "Very fast," in his strong German accent, before sinking beneath the surface and returning to his lane.

We met again the following night. I earned my first gold at the Games, breaking my world record, and Roland won the bronze behind my U.S. teammate Peter Rocca. Roland had been "the man to beat" for a remarkable eight years after setting his first world record.

Standing on the awards stand, Roland was surprisingly charming and gracious. But it was his semifinal comment that I treasure the most. The man I idolized told me that he was *impressed by me*. Roland's compliment impacted me for life.

We can use our words to build walls or to be a force of influence. Who can you bless with a few words of encouragement today?

A word aptly spoken is like apples of gold in settings of silver.
PROVERBS 25:11

21

Lost and Found Promises

Madeline Manning Mims
U.S. Olympic Gold Medalist in Track

You and I can never be sure of what will happen or not happen in this world, but we can be absolutely sure of the utter faithfulness of the One who made it and engineers all things according to His glorious promises.

ELISABETH ELLIOT

What do you do when that which has been so precious to your heart turns out to be the very thing that nearly destroys you?

Last year I had a rude awakening. Up until then, I had enjoyed the best days of my life in a marriage that seemed made in heaven. It had been tried in the fiery trials of life, strengthened and made stable, but then everything went suddenly, horribly wrong. Overnight my sanctuary of a strong, healthy family seemed to be irretrievably broken. I was devastated!

I wondered, *Did I miss God speaking to me about the promise of a mate who would join with me to finish the work I was called to in the earth for His purpose? How could I have been so wrong about the promises God had spoken to my heart?* I lost hope, faith and the promise I thought I had heard from God.

One thing I didn't let go of was my *trust* in God for my life. What else did I have to hold on to? Fame, medals, world records, money (or the lack thereof), position, influence and even admiration had done nothing to stop this from happening. Still, I knew that no matter what, God loved me and had my best at heart. He was the only One who could get me through this without me losing my mind (which was a little on the scrambled side right about then).

I held on to the Scripture that promises, "Trust in the LORD with all your heart and lean not on your own understanding; in all your ways acknowledge him and he will make your paths straight" (Proverbs 3:5-6). As I grasped this word and tearfully surrendered to its truth, strength, hope and peace began to flood my ravaged soul. I began to heal and take the next step to wholeness, one day at a time.

In the end, the petals of my life fell to the ground to be used as fertilizer for the budding seeds of spring. God has not only put back together the broken pieces of my life, but He has also made all things new in a relationship that had ceased to exist.

If you have watched your dreams become dust before your eyes, say this prayer with me:

Father God, thank You for being here for me through the good and the bad in my life. Thank You for protecting me from the destruction Satan had planned for me. I will surrender my trust and faith into Your strong hands of protection over my soul. You have carried me through the valley of the shadow of death; therefore I fear no evil. My life is lost in Your will, to be found again in Your glory through Jesus Christ, my Savior and Lord. Amen.

Through these he has given us his very great and precious promises . . .
2 PETER 1:4

22

Friendships Are Golden

John Naber
Four-time U.S. Olympic Gold Medalist in Swimming

Shared joy is a double joy; shared sorrow is half a sorrow.
SWEDISH PROVERB

At the 1976 Olympics in Montreal, Canada, my teammate Bruce Furniss was the pre-meet favorite in the 200-meter freestyle. Bruce and I had been workout partners at the University of Southern California for two years. During practice, I pushed him when he got tired and he returned the favor when I ran out of steam. Since my nickname was "Snake," he naturally took the moniker "Mongoose." Not predators or competitors, we called each other "compreditors." We joked a lot and enjoyed each other's companionship.

Perhaps it's not strange that the Games create moments of meaning, but it is unusual for two such close friends to compete against each other. As the slowest qualifier into the finals, I swam my race in the outside lane. Bruce was the top qualifier and earned the center lane. Somehow, I made it a close race.

In the finals of the 200-meter freestyle, Keith Jackson boomed into his ABC television headset microphone, "As they come to the wall, it's Naber, it's Naber, it's Naber, it's . . . Furniss . . . with a new world record of 1:50:29."

Interestingly, I viewed my second-place finish as an unexpected blessing, not a failure. I knew the Lord wanted me to celebrate my friend's victory. Following the finish of the race, I swam under the lane ropes that separated us and gave Bruce a big hug and a smile. Both Bruce and I had bettered the existing world record. The United States had "swept" the top three places. We finished first and second and stood next to each other on the award stand.

Later, after the mandatory press conference and drug testing, we headed out to meet our parents for dinner. Walking beneath the bleachers, we came across the warm-down pool.

"You know, John," Bruce began, "we didn't have time to loosen down after our race, and tomorrow we have the finals of the 800-meter free relay. Perhaps it would be a good idea if we took a moment to swim off the race." I agreed.

We quickly stripped off our sweat suits and jumped into the pool, slowly swimming side by side down the length of the pool. After 175 meters, we were both ideally loose and relaxed. Bruce looked at the wall 25 meters away and smiled, asking, "Do you wanna race?"

Less than an hour earlier, he and I had pushed each other to go the distance faster than anyone on the planet had done before. The cameras and eyes of the world had witnessed the feat, and the awards had been placed around our necks. *Now, in the solitude of an empty warm-down pool*, I said to myself, *he's asking me if I want to race?*

"Come on, now, Bruce," I slowly sighed. "I don't think we have anything else to prove . . ." *and I took off!* By surprising him, I jumped out to a quick, half-body-length lead, but as I reached for the wall, I felt his hand grab the waist of my swim trunks and pull me back. Laughing out loud, we wrestled our way to the edge of the water.

Long after the race, our friendship lingers. And our private race is still my favorite memory from those Games.

Do you have friends that are as good as gold? Or are you so competitive that you miss the joys of friendship?

As iron sharpens iron, so one man sharpens another.
PROVERBS 27:17

2 3

A Labor of Love

Leah O'Brien-Amico
Three-time U.S. Olympic Softball Team Gold Medalist

What the heart gives away is never gone . . .
It is kept in the hearts of others.
Robin St. John

As a professional female athlete, I faced a dilemma. I wanted to be a mom. But I still wanted to compete for my country. A pregnancy required a break from rigorous training. But I knew there were no guarantees—I could still get cut from the team, even if I weren't pregnant. Carefully weighing the consequences, my husband, Tommy, and I decided not to delay starting a family after I won my second Olympic gold medal in Sydney.

So I pioneered uncharted waters when my first son, Jake, was born, and I became the first mom on the U.S. softball team. Each morning I'd wake up—sometimes after a sleepless night comforting my crying baby—get the baby fed and ready, pack a lunch, drop the baby off, work out and then pick Jake up.

I couldn't have done it without my husband and my mother. The three of us played tag team. As a working mom, at least I was only separated from our son a few hours a day while I was training locally.

Traveling was tricky. When we flew to tournaments, I took Jake with me and arranged for a friend to fly with me to babysit while I played. Jake was the first baby to travel on our team's bus tours. He lightened things up and helped us keep life in perspective on the road.

I'll never forget walking off the field after one particularly terrible game. Jake ran up to me and wrapped his little fingers around my neck in a big hug. His unconditional love reminded me it was just a game. When my team went to Italy for three weeks, I cried when I had to leave him behind.

In continuing to play after having a baby, I set a precedent. Now three of my teammates have babies and are still playing instead of postponing the joys of motherhood. Although I'm retired, I still lead softball clinics on weekends.

In the midst of our busy family schedule, I have to be more purposeful to prioritize my relationship with God. Here are some tips I've found:

- Get plugged in to a good local church.
- Play Christian music while running errands with the kids.
- Pray out loud together as a family.
- Consider homeschooling. I'm teaching Jake with a Christian curriculum.
- Put Bible verses on the refrigerator as reminders of what is really important.
- Refuel with God's Word, Proverbs in particular, for a few minutes each day.
- Surround your family with other Christian families.

Yes, being a mom to three young boys is a real balancing act, but I wouldn't trade it for the world. Take a look at your goals and your desires. What kind of life are you striving to have? What are you doing to prioritize God and relationships in your daily life?

Sons are a heritage from the LORD, children a reward from him.
PSALM 127:3

24

Daily Bread

Ruth Riley
U.S. Olympic Basketball Team Gold Medalist

I shall walk this way but only once. Therefore whatever good I might do let me do it now, for I shall never walk this way again.
SOURCE UNKNOWN

My spiritual life has been a journey. Growing up in a single-parent home wasn't easy. But my mom never stopped encouraging me in my faith. She took me to Sunday School, even though I didn't always want to be there. It wasn't until I enrolled at the University of Notre Dame that I started to really embrace my faith as my own.

My beliefs and convictions grew even stronger when I moved to Miami to play in the WNBA. Pregame chapel meetings and Bible studies with my teammates gave me a *hunger* for God's Word. I was just hungry in a spiritual sense though. Little did I know that God would soon show me a new meaning of "hunger."

In 2006, I traveled to Africa as a spokesperson for Nothing But Nets, an organization that prevents the spread of malaria through the use of mosquito nets. Nearly 3,000 kids die every day in Africa from malaria. More deadly than AIDS, malaria continues to ravage the continent of Africa. According to the World Health Organization, the use of mosquito bed nets and prompt treatment could reduce the malaria transmission rate by 60 percent. A net costing about $10 can cover a family of four for about four years.

During my time in Africa, I was also deeply moved by the ever-present problem of hunger and malnutrition. Many Africans are dying from starvation. The fact is, many of us will never really know what it means to be physically hungry. We live in a "fast-food nation," where a burger and fries can be found on every street corner. Yet there are millions in this world—and in the U.S.—who have plenty to eat physically but are starving spiritually.

I was so inspired by the Christian faith I saw in those in Africa who weren't sure when their next meal would come. I heard a beautiful story from a woman in Nigeria who shared that she had recently lost a child to malaria. When I asked her if she feared losing any more of her children to this disease, she simply said, "No, I believe in God." Her faith, a strong and unwavering faith, is what sustains her. On a continent that seems stuck in a hopeless cycle of poverty and disease, I discovered that its people still find hope through the "bread of life" found only in God's promises.

What do you fill the emptiness in your heart with? Money? Status? Relationships? Though these things may be temporarily satisfying, an aching hunger and sickness remain without the love of Jesus Christ.

I pray that today you seek out ways to serve others less fortunate than you, and that you eat the spiritual "bread of life" that Jesus offers to you.

For I was hungry and you gave me something to eat . . .
I was sick and you looked after me.
MATTHEW 25:35-36

Then Jesus declared, "I am the bread of life. He who comes to me will
never go hungry, and he who believes in me will never be thirsty."
JOHN 6:35

Forgiven to Forgive

Congressman Jim Ryun
U.S. Olympic Silver Medalist in the 1500-Meter Run

*Forgiving and being forgiven are experiences that
allow me to be free for a new day.*
MARTIN MARTY

For 10 years, running was my god. I gave my god the best of everything—my time, my energy, my love. At the age of 25, however, I realized something was missing in my life. According to the world's
standards, I was very successful. I was the world record holder in
the mile, had been on the cover of *Sports Illustrated* and still had
many years of running left in my legs.

Success according to the world's barometer was nice, but there
was a great emptiness within me. No matter how fast I ran, people
were always expecting more. No matter how many awards I won, I
always wanted more. There was no peace inside, and at times living
seemed more like a roller-coaster ride than a rewarding journey.

I had been raised in a church and, while growing up, was literally there every time the church doors were open. But I didn't
know what it meant to have a personal relationship with a living
Savior until, on May 18, 1972, my wife, Anne, and I gave our lives
to Christ. Accepting Christ meant that we both acknowledged a
change in our priorities.

Not long after, I was America's hope for the gold in the 1500-
meter race at the 1972 Olympics in Munich, Germany. That hope

died when I fell 500 meters short of the finish line in my qualifying race. Though the video proved I had been fouled, the Olympic Committee refused to reinstate me.

"Lord," I complained, "these officials know I was fouled. They won't reinstate me because they've never done such a thing before."

I had focused all my training and energy for a full year on that one event. Now it had been stolen from me. The old Jim Ryun wanted to express his anger to each committee member with a swift kick of his size 12½ track shoe. But how was the new Christian Jim Ryun going to handle the situation?

It would be nice to say that the Lord performed a miracle and got me back in the race. Instead, He decided on a greater miracle.

For years, I struggled with hurt and bitterness over that event. One night, I knelt and said, "Lord, forgive me for the bitterness in my heart." I knew the Lord had forgiven me, but I still felt unable to forgive those who had wronged me.

I continued in prayer, pursuing complete forgiveness. Then one day, I became aware of an amazing thing: I was no longer bitter. It had been a process. It's hard work to forgive because it is not a one-shot deal. But I had made the decision to forgive. It was my choice, and I worked through it over a long period of time through prayer, Bible study, and the support and encouragement of other believers.

God allowed me to be disqualified from the world's most prestigious athletic competition to show me how to be a real winner.

Have you been wronged or treated unjustly? Is bitterness from a past hurt still wounding you today? Just as He forgives us, He frees us to forgive others, even when we're treated unfairly. If you are harboring bitterness in your heart, ask the Lord to begin the healing process today. Freedom is sweet indeed.

If you hold anything against anyone, forgive him, so that your Father in heaven may forgive you your sins.
MARK 11:25

The Blessed Life

Gabe Woodward
U.S. Olympic Swimming Team

In the dust of defeat as well as in the laurels of victory
there is a glory to be found if one has done his best!
ERIC LIDDELL

We all try our best to be blessed. But it helps to have the correct definition of what "blessed" means.

After a pretty good college career, I had a dream of competing at the Games, getting married and working in finance like many of the other men in my family. About that time, I suffered a shoulder injury that almost paralyzed my right arm. In this place of surrender, I signed up for classes in biblical counseling at The Master's College just so I could learn what a blessed life really looks like.

I attended seminary for a year and Psalm 1 was my daily prayer. After a semester of much growth at Master's, I met an amazing Christian woman, Staci. We got married later that year. Then I tried my hand at finance to provide for my new wife. That didn't work out very well—I failed the first round of tests and my first boss fired me. Thankfully, my arm had finally healed and Staci agreed to help me train for the Olympics. It was a long shot, but we knew that if God was at the center of our lives, we would be blessed, no matter what the outcome.

Finally, when I was 25—and the underdog—God allowed me to make the 2004 swim team in the 4x100 freestyle relay. When I came home with the bronze medal, I passed my financial advisor exam, and we found out that Staci was pregnant with our first child.

Yes, I am a blessed man. But I was blessed before I was married, before I was an Olympian and even before I had a job, because I had Jesus Christ in my life. When God's Word and His presence in your life are your delight, and you seek first His kingdom, you will be blessed!

What is your definition of being blessed? Will you trust God to give you the best He has for you in His timing?

How blessed is the man who does not walk in the counsel
of the wicked. . . . But his delight is in the law of the LORD,
and on His law he meditates day and night. He is like a tree
planted by the streams of water, which yields its fruit in season. . . .
Whatever he does prospers.
PSALM 1:1-3

Blessed are all who fear the LORD, who walk in his ways.
You will eat the fruit of your labor; blessings and prosperity will be
yours. Your wife will be like a fruitful vine within your house.
PSALM 128:1-3

27

Spiritual Strength

Brandon Slay
Olympic Gold Medalist in Wrestling

It makes no sense to seek your God-given strength until you trust in his.
MAX LUCADO

For many years, I attempted to accomplish my wrestling dreams without God. I relied only on my own mental and physical strength. I pushed my body every day to the limit in training, and I thoroughly analyzed my opponent's moves before each match. While I had outstanding success, I could only get so far. In 1999, my own strength led me to only a sixth-place finish at the U.S. Nationals. Not knowing what more I could have done, I questioned myself.

When a pastor asked me what my purpose in life was, I was embarrassed to admit that I really didn't have one. Finally forced to analyze myself, I realized that my life was just a black hole of self-centeredness and pleasure-seeking. Losing at Nationals had made me angry at myself—and even more driven to make myself feel good through partying. That, of course, wasn't going to help me train any better either. I was a mess!

Deep down I knew what my purpose should have been: to follow Jesus. Every year as a kid I went to the evangelistic outreach put on by the Power Team. These mighty Christian weightlifters showed us incredible feats of muscular strength, and then told us that the greatest act of strength was Jesus' dying for our sins. And every year I went down front and prayed to commit my life to Jesus.

But then I got older, got good at sports and got caught up with girls. As I gave myself over to the lust of the eye and the pride of life, I lost my connection to God.

When I finally got right with Jesus, I at last found what was missing—spiritual strength. The Bible tells us that the "joy of the LORD is your strength" (Nehemiah 8:10). When joy in Jesus finally replaced my inner emptiness, I found the power to persevere, pushing myself until I developed my full God-given potential as an athlete and as a person.

Moments after becoming one of the first Texans to make the wrestling team for the 2000 Summer Olympics, a reporter ran up to me with a microphone and asked, "I just want to know, where do you draw your strength from?" As the crowd quietly waited for my response, I testified, "I draw my strength from my Lord and Savior Jesus Christ." It was an emotional moment as the stadium erupted with applause for about 40 seconds.

With my new spiritual foundation, at Sydney I moved from sixth in the United States to first in the world. Jesus had helped me sort out my personal life so that I could finally fully focus on developing my potential as an athlete.

Coming home to Jesus won't ensure that you will be a big winner in sports, but Christ will make you a winner in life. You will find lasting joy in His love. And when you are winning in life, you don't care how your best compares with others.

Are you winning in life?

"Not by might nor by power but by my Spirit,"
says the LORD Almighty.
ZECHARIAH 4:6

Humbling Challenges

Cat Reddick Whitehill
U.S. Olympic Soccer Team Gold Medalist

*If you are humble nothing will touch you, neither praise nor disgrace,
because you know who you are.*
MOTHER TERESA

My soccer career has been sprinkled with seasons of humility. Sure, I've reached the summits of my sport—NCAA Championship, Olympic gold medal, World Cup bronze medal—but it has most often been through moments of humility and failure that God has reminded me of His infinite love and faithfulness.

Leading up to college, I was one of the top high school soccer players in the country. My team in Birmingham, Alabama, won four consecutive state titles, and I was a highly touted recruit. I eventually accepted a scholarship to play for the University of North Carolina, where I was promised a starting defensive position.

Although my high school team was one of the best in the country, I soon realized the level of play at UNC was faster and stronger than what I was accustomed to. My skills and conditioning needed improvement, so my coach decided to start a "walk on" player in front of me.

I spent that season discouraged, frustrated and humbled. I turned to my family for support, relying heavily on the lessons of perseverance they had taught me as a child. My family had always modeled a life of dependency on Christ. Therefore, I felt a deep sense of loss without them. The only comfort I had going into college was the expectation of being a starter on one of the best teams in the country—and now that was gone. I was devastated!

During that dark time, my own perseverance wasn't enough—I needed God. Dropping to my knees, I asked for help. The foundational truth of Psalm 3:3 eventually gave me the freedom to be my very best: "But you, O LORD, are a shield about me, my glory, and the one who lifts my head."

By the end of the season, I had earned my starting position back for *one* game—the National Championship! Our team went on to win, and I was named the MVP! God had given me strength when I was at my weakest. His strength gave me the freedom to triumph.

Did you know that Jesus carried out the greatest act of humility? The book of Philippians says that Jesus "humbled himself and became obedient to death" (2:8). If the God of the universe humbled Himself to become a man and then sacrificed His own life to demonstrate how much He loves me, shouldn't I be able to demonstrate humility in my own life?

Throughout the Bible, God's people are often taken through humbling circumstances. God often allows us to be humbled to remind us of our great need for Him.

Are you willing to receive God's love during moments of humility? My prayer is that you will allow God to lift you "out of the slimy pit" of discouragement and set your "feet on a rock" of grace today (see Psalm 40).

But you are a shield around me, O LORD; you bestow glory
on me and lift up my head.
PSALM 3:3

29

Staying in the Game

Krystal Thomas
Duke Basketball Player
Member of U.S.A. U-19 Team

Success is to be measured not so much by the position that one has reached as by the obstacles which have been overcome while trying to succeed.
BOOKER T. WASHINGTON

My life hasn't been easy. I started playing basketball in fifth grade, but battled injuries until eighth grade. I looked up to my parents. When my dad, a respected Orange County Deputy, was arrested for trafficking stolen goods when I was 11, our lives changed overnight.

Three months after my dad's imprisonment, my mom was diagnosed with stage-4 breast cancer. At that point, I faced the responsibility of helping raise my four younger siblings on top of school and basketball practice. I learned to drive at age 14 and drove by myself at 15 out of necessity. Thankfully, mom's cancer went into remission.

Things seemed to be turning around. Mom was better, and in my sophomore year in high school, top college recruiters started scouting me. Sadly, however, Mom's cancer returned.

Despite her illness, Mom came to every game and most practices, even after chemotherapy. Not only was she an inspiration to my family, but also to my team and the entire school. My church and school community pitched in to coordinate meals, care for my mom, help with babysitting and oversee homework for my siblings while my sister and teammate, Loren, and I practiced.

Mom's health rapidly declined. My junior year, she was only able to attend the first three games of our season. We prayed that my mom would be able to attend the dedication ceremony for our school's new gym on December 13, 2006. I was so proud when they named the Natalie Thomas Gymnasium after her and everyone honored her with a standing ovation. Although visibly exhausted, Mom stayed to cheer us on for a few minutes. That was her last game.

Tragically, Mom passed away in January, right before our basketball playoffs. At her memorial service, I encouraged everyone, "She has the best seat in the house now!" I deeply missed my mom cheering me on at games, but God's comfort gave me the strength to make it, both on the court and in life.

With my dad still in jail, one of my mom's last wishes was that the five of us children wouldn't be split up. My mom's prayers were answered when our teammate Alexa and her parents, Don and Sheri Deluzio, compassionately offered to take all of us into their home, even though they already had four children. They were like angels, opening their hearts and home to us and completely rearranging their lives to make us feel welcome.

As we prepared for the state championship later that year, each of my teammates had my mom's initials, "NT," embroidered on a patch on the back of her jersey. I led my team to win the state championship title for my mom, followed by a second state championship my senior year. I knew Mom watched from above, and it was special having my sister on both teams.

At my senior team banquet, I thought of Mom. She was still my hero. I looked up to her for everything. Amazingly, no matter how difficult her circumstances grew, she never seemed to lose heart and faithfully trusted in God. Her perseverance made anything I experienced seem bearable.

John 16:33 warns us that we will face many troubles on Earth—the secret is to take heart, knowing He has already overcome.

No matter what difficulties you are facing in life, don't ever let them keep you down or stop you. Through my trials, I've experienced God's faithfulness. He can bring you through every difficult circumstance. Look to Him for strength today!

We are hard pressed on every side, but not crushed; perplexed, but not in despair.

2 CORINTHIANS 4:8

30

Unifying Hope

Laura Wilkinson
U.S. Olympic Gold Medalist in Diving

Hope is the essential ingredient to make it through life.
It is the anchor of the soul.
BARBARA JOHNSON

At the Games, champions are born, heroes are made, and the stories behind the headlines are written on our hearts. While precious few taste the sweetness of a medal, most stumble, watching their dreams fade.

But there is one factor, one promise, one reason that motivates elite athletes to unite every four years for a common goal. It's actually quite simple. It's *hope*.

It's bittersweet preparing for 2008 in Beijing, my third and final Olympics before retiring. Traveling to the diving stronghold of the world to compete against a dominant Chinese team in their own backyard, I have no idea what is about to unfold. But I have hope that I can put my whole heart into each dive. Hope that anyone—even me, at twice the age of my wide-eyed teen competitors—can overcome injuries and seemingly impossible odds.

I have hope . . . and God's hope does not disappoint.

"Now faith is the assurance of things hoped for, the conviction of things not seen" (Hebrews 11:1, *NASB*). This verse is not a definition of faith, like I used to think. It is a *description* of it. In my study Bible, it says that in this verse, faith treats things *hoped for* as reality. Faith itself proves that what is unseen is real.

We all tend to prefer facts and scientific proof. We've all heard the line, "When I see it, I'll believe it." At the Games, the complete opposite is true. Not one of us would be there if we didn't believe in our potential. As athletes trying to win a medal, we *must* believe in ourselves before we see results. As athletes, we have great faith in our own abilities, and tremendous hope.

But I also know that in whatever place I end up—first or last—God will use that to glorify Himself and shape my character. My teammate Kimiko put it beautifully: "You don't have faith so that you can get what you want. You have faith for who He is."

Yes, I pursue excellence because I want to win again. But I know that I don't need a gold medal or a certain score to know that I'm significant.

We each matter because God made everyone unique and special. No collection of titles, medals, degrees or money can give us that. We can put our hope in Jeremiah 29:11, where God says that He has plans for us, not to harm us, but to give us hope and a future!

As I turn 30, everything is stacked against me in Beijing. I'm nervous but also excited because I get to hang on to God. My heart is filled with peace, knowing that God has called me to this place for His plan. My weaknesses are God's opportunity to showcase His strength and glory to the world. I know that He is with me and will never leave me—that is the best *hope* that I have ever known.

Is your hope in God alone (see Psalm 62:5)? Or are you putting your hope in your dreams, job, talents, popularity or other things that are temporary?

May the God of hope fill you with all joy and peace as you trust in him,
so that you may overflow with hope by the power of the Holy Spirit.
ROMANS 15:13

Temporary Amnesia

Annett Davis
U.S. Olympic Beach Volleyball Team

When the big decisions really come down to the moment of truth,
do you really believe that God will care for you?
DR. DAVID JEREMIAH

Do you recall the story of God parting the Red Sea, saving the Israelites from the Egyptians? How about God instructing a man named Noah to build a boat, because the world was so evil that He was going to destroy it with a flood? What about Jesus teaching 5,000 hungry people and performing a miracle by feeding them with only 5 loaves of bread and 2 fish?

These are some of the more popular stories of the Bible that we've heard many times. Stories of God's love, His mercy, His grace and His provision. Hundreds of pages in the Bible remind us of who God is and all He's done for us.

I've experienced several financially challenging times in my life. While I was qualifying for the 2000 Olympics, costly international travel to mandatory volleyball competitions created a financial burden that almost stopped me from reaching my dream. Remembering that He gave manna to the Israelites, fed the 5,000 and even takes care of the birds, I believed that *surely* He'd take care of me. Standing on the promises of God's provision, I prayed that His will would be done. God faithfully provided my airfare and expenses from sponsors, friends, family and other unexpected sources.

Reading the Bible, I've noticed that God's people often had a problem with short-term memory. Right after God had miraculously intervened on their behalf, they would doubt that He could do it again the next time they faced a similar sticky situation. It was like they suffered from a case of temporary amnesia. I've promised myself that I'll make every effort not to forget what God has done for me.

Here are some ways I've discovered that we as Christians can reflect on God's faithfulness:

- Memorize Scriptures that pertain to your situation, and write verses on note cards. Place them around the house as reminders.
- Share with others your own personal stories of what wonderful things God has done.
- Journal it!
- When you overcome an addiction, write a victory note in your Outlook, Palm or Treo and have it come up as a reminder alarm once a month.
- Schedule daily praise time, even if it's only a few minutes.

God deserves the glory, and we should never forget what He has done for us. Recalling how God brought me through past needs reminds me that He is capable of doing it again if He chooses. Either way, I will still praise Him.

Are you suffering from temporary amnesia? Take a moment to think about the times God has brought you through a need. Then make an act of faith, declaring that you will trust God with any challenges you are currently facing.

I will remember the deeds of the LORD;
yes, I will remember your miracles of long ago.
PSALM 77:11

More than Medals

Jennie Finch
Three-time U.S. Olympic Gold Medalist in Softball

Wealth stays with us a little moment if at all: only our characters are steadfast, not our gold.
EURIPIDES

Our hands grasped together tightly, my softball teammates and I stepped up onto the center podium in unison. We waved to our families, friends and the incredible fans that had supported us throughout the long journey. As I turned once again to look into the smiling faces of my teammates around me, the reality of the moment finally started to sink in. After beating our main rival (Australia) in the finals, we were champions for the third consecutive Olympic Games.

The dream that had followed me since I was old enough to pick up a bat and ball had finally become true! I was an Olympic gold medalist. I began to think about all the sacrifices, hard work, love and commitment that had made this moment possible.

Next, my gaze drifted down to the field where our head coach was standing. Embracing his daughter, Coach Mike Candrea looked up and locked eyes with each and every one of us. As his eyes met mine, I could see the emotions in his face: joy, relief . . . and sadness.

A month earlier, our softball family was rocked when Coach Candrea's wife, Sue, died of a brain aneurism. My college coach at the University of Arizona and now our National Team coach, Coach Candrea lost not only his wife, but also his best friend. Had he decided to withdraw from the Games, any one of us would have understood.

However, he knew that if Sue were still alive, she would want nothing more than for her husband to lead his team in Athens. So, with courage and grace, he led us to a perfect 9-0 Olympic record as we outscored our opponents 51-1 en route to the gold.

As the medal was placed around my neck, I silently thanked God and Coach Candrea for reminding me that life is more than medals, more than winning—even more than the game I've loved playing since I was five years old. Life is about investing in people, as Coach Candrea and his wife have invested in me. Life is about my family, my friends and my teammates. Life is about my relationship with Jesus Christ. I know that investing in these relationships will always have a huge return.

Since winning the gold in Athens, I've been approached by *FHM* and other men's magazines for money-making opportunities. Although making money and having influence can be tempting, God's rewards for taking the narrow path are greater than any financial gains the world can offer.

Are you sacrificing your relationships for the sake of your goals? Have you stopped investing in people and started investing in things? Will you allow God to reward you with His greater blessing as you fight the temptation to forfeit your relationships for the pursuit of a goal?

Teach us to number our days and recognize how few they are;
help us to spend them as we should.
PSALM 90:12, *TLB*

A Heart of Thankfulness

Annett Davis
U.S. Olympic Beach Volleyball Team

Hem your blessings with thankfulness so they don't unravel.
AUTHOR UNKNOWN

Leading up to the 2000 Games, my teammate and I were battling through the long process of qualification. In beach volleyball, that's a two-year process. I was married and had one child at the time, so traveling the world was fun and exciting but I desperately missed my family at home.

During one trip, we had been in France for two weeks already, and I was so ready to get home. We almost missed a mandatory players' meeting because I had written down the wrong time. If we had missed this meeting, we would have been sent home early along with our aspirations to compete in the Games. Then, on the first day of competition, we nearly lost our first two games. But miraculously, God brought us through and we continued to advance through the tournament field.

On the night before the Sunday final, I was selfishly griping because I was ready to see my family. Our original flight had been scheduled to depart that night, but because we had made the finals on Sunday, the airline told us they would not be able to get us out until Monday or Tuesday.

"Are you kidding me? Why?!" I asked out loud in frustration.

I remember the quiet voice of God replying, "Why ask 'why?'

Why not say 'thank You'? Don't you know all I do for you?"

Like a child who had been scolded by her daddy, I just closed my mouth and repented. How ungrateful I had been! God had done so much for me, and it still wasn't enough! In the finals, we played one of our best matches en route to taking home the title . . . but the story doesn't end there.

We rushed to the airport after the finals on Sunday, but the airline staff said we would not make it on the flight that day because we were too far down on the waiting list. Minutes before the flight took off, however, an airline representative called us over, handed us two tickets and said, "Enjoy your flight."

Then, as we boarded the plane, we expected to be sitting in coach, which was fine with us because we were so thankful to be going home. Well, we were immediately directed to upper-deck seats—in business class! This was clearly a gift from God. We had purchased economy class seats and neither of us had built up any privileges with this airline. So, as I ate my steak and reclined my seat to the full "bed" position, this prayer filled my heart, "All I do, I do for You."

God does so much on our behalf. Will you use today to say, "Thank You"? Ask God to forgive you for those times when you have taken His generosity and love for granted.

So then, just as you received Christ Jesus as Lord, continue to live in him, rooted and built up in him, strengthened in the faith as you were taught, and overflowing with thankfulness.

COLOSSIANS 2:6-7

3 4

Hearing God Through the Silence

Vonetta Flowers
U.S. Olympic Gold Medalist in Bobsledding

Faith makes things possible, not easy.
AUTHOR UNKNOWN

February 19, 2002. As I stepped up onto the Salt Lake City Olympic Games gold medal platform amid deafening chants of, "U.S.A.! U.S.A.! U.S.A.!" I thought of all my friends and family back home in Birmingham, Alabama, who were screaming and yelling at the television set as their track-star-converted-bobsledder became the first black athlete from any nation to win gold at a Winter Games.

The cheers echoed in my ears long after the medal was draped around my neck. But what if you couldn't physically *hear* the roar of a crowd? What would life be like in a silent world? Could you still "hear" the voice of God?

Six months after the Salt Lake City Games, I gave birth to fraternal twins, Jorden and Jaden. Although my precious sons were born 10 weeks early and weighed less than 3 pounds each, Jaden's physical development appeared normal. However, Jorden was born with no ear canals or auditory nerves, leaving him completely deaf.

After several unsuccessful attempts with hearing aids, my husband and I flew Jorden to Italy to meet with renowned surgeon Dr. Vittorio Coletti. He is currently the only one in the world performing a groundbreaking auditory brain stem implant surgery. After meeting with Dr. Coletti, and after much prayer, we decided to give Jorden a chance to hear for the very first time. He would become the first American child and one of only a few worldwide to undergo this experimental procedure. Dr. Coletti and his team implanted electrodes on part of Jorden's brain to stimulate his hearing pathway, allowing sound to be sent to our son's brain.

Well, God worked a miracle! Although we did not experience a made-for-Hollywood moment immediately after surgery, Jorden's steady progress is nothing short of extraordinary. Two years ago, he was 100-percent deaf. Today, after the successful surgery and work with speech therapists in Birmingham and Jacksonville, five-year-old Jorden responds to our voices and is learning to speak for the first time. And thanks to University of Florida medical artists and doctors at the Children's Hospital of Alabama, he is one of the youngest patients to enjoy prosthetic ears.

The procedure itself cost more than $60,000 and wasn't covered by insurance because it's not an approved procedure in the U.S. yet. So we needed a financial miracle. Thankfully, Dr. Coletti donated his services. We've been extremely blessed to have so many wonderful supporters, like Allianz Life Insurance Company, our church (Faith Chapel Christian Center) and so many others who have helped and encouraged us throughout this journey. Because of their generous support and God's unfailing love and mercy our son's life has been forever changed.

A couple of weeks ago, Jorden turned to me and said, "I love you, Mommy." My heart was filled with joy because when I replied, "I love you too, Jorden," his smile was enough for me to know that he could hear me.

Every day God is waiting to communicate His love to us. Are you tuning in and listening for your heavenly Father's voice?

His sheep follow him because they know his voice.

JOHN 10:4

3 5

Never Alone

Matt Scoggin
U.S. Olympic Diving Team

God loves each of us as if there were only one of us.
St. Augustine

At the U.S. National Diving Championships in Indianapolis in April 1992, I was supposed to show everyone that I was the man to beat in the Barcelona Olympic trials two months later. The previous year had been the best training year of my life, and it was all on my shoulders to prove that I was the best. There was no doubt that I had done everything I could do to win. To my utter shock and disappointment, I finished in fifth place. I couldn't understand why things didn't work out like I had planned them.

Later that night, my wife, Becca, and I were eating a salad at Wendy's. She could tell I was upset and gave me some life-changing advice: "Matt, you need to continue training with this same intensity, but you also need to know that you're not alone. There's an old saying, 'Work like it's up to you, and pray like it's all up to God.' The truth is, Matt, you've got to believe that God will give you a peace and a power that you can't achieve on your own. In fact, He gives you His very presence! Remember, Someone very powerful is with you. You're not alone."

Sure enough, she was right! When I competed at the Olympic trials two months later, I asked God to help me and then trusted that He was right there with me. The confident peace He gave me allowed me to be relaxed yet aggressive, enjoying the moment while maintaining my focus. Knowing that I was never alone as I dove off that 10-meter platform released me to be my very best. I ended up winning the trials by a landslide and qualifying for the Barcelona team.

That experience was, in a way, the beginning of my spiritual journey. God has continued to reveal His goodness and grace to my wife and me in so many ways. In fact, we even named our daughter "Grace," in light of the grace God continues to show us.

That day was a turning point for my parents, as well. At the invitation of some friends, they went to church for the first time in decades before the diving finals. As he was praying, my dad, Phil, turned to my mom and said, "Joannie, if Matt makes the team, we need to start going to church." Well, they've been going to church ever since. They know, like I do, that God does answer prayer—and we're never alone!

My advice to you: (1) marry an awesome Christian like I did, and (2) remember you're never alone!

How are you acknowledging the presence of God in your daily circumstances? Are you humbling yourself and leaning on His strength and wisdom?

And surely I am with you always, to the very end of the age.
MATTHEW 28:20

The Victory of Love: Live Righteously—Radiate Love

Eric Liddell
Scottish Olympic Gold Medalist in Track

God, who foresaw your tribulation, has specially armed you to go through it, not with out pain but without stain.

C. S. LEWIS

God does not say that because you believe in Him, He will keep you from hardship and suffering. He says that if you trust Him, He will strengthen you to meet all the experiences of life in a conquering spirit. You will have secret resources of power to call on when they are needed.

Life is full of hard experiences, bitter disappointments, unexpected losses, grim tragedies. How do Christians face these? Here are several thoughts that may help.

Evil comes not from God but through the sin, malice, callousness, passions, selfishness and neglect of people. God is not responsible for these.

There are also disasters, calamities and accidents which are the other side of the privilege and joy of living in a world such as this. If there were no spice of risk, there would be no zest of adventure.

Sometimes evil comes through the direct malice of people. It is easy to harbor feelings of hate, a desire to be God's instrument of vengeance. It is a terrible thing to fall into the hands of a hate like that. For hate desolates both the wronged and the wrongdoer.

This work of punishment is not ours but God's.

It is a perilous position for anyone to claim to be the instrument of the judgment of God. God is working in the hearts of those who have wronged us as well as in our hearts. His mills are grinding out restlessly the judgments of righteousness. Leave all to God. The justice of God is far more sure and unerring, for it is the justice of love, a love that will not let people go, but follows them still through all the mazes of their flight from it, till it brings them to redemption. It is this vision of God behind the scenes that calms the heart and takes away the restless heat of rancor and revenge. It helps one to face all in a magnanimous spirit.

Circumstances may appear to wreck our lives and God's plans, but God is not helpless among the ruins. Our broken lives are not lost or useless. God's love is still working. He comes in and takes the calamity and uses it victoriously, working out His wonderful plan of love. "All things work together for good to them that love God." He is always master of the situation. There is infinite resourcefulness in the almighty love. Many people have become great in spite of, as well as because of, disaster. This is the victory of God's love, but it does not come to all. It comes to those who keep their faith clear and their lives clean toward God. It comes to those who keep in touch with the divine love, are linked to the divine will and look for chances of helping on the purposes they are sure God still has for them.

When you pass through the waters, I will be with you.
ISAIAH 43:2

This is the victory that has overcome the world.
1 JOHN 5:4

From Eric Liddell, *The Disciplines of the Christian Life* (Nashville, TN: Abingdon Press, 1985). Used by permission.

Conclusion

I never tire of these amazing stories of courage. Like Matt Hemingway, jumping higher than ever while working a full-time job to provide for his family. Or Krystal Thomas, who didn't quit basketball and maintained a 3.8 G.P.A. while helping raise her four younger siblings, despite her dad going to jail and her mom dying of cancer. These and all the other Christian athletes whose testimonies we've read definitely had guts!

Do you need to be a Christian to have guts? Certainly there are some motivated, successful people out there who don't consider the Source of their gifts. And the very thought of leaning on God is downright offensive—or at best irrelevant—to some.

But I say that the best motivation, the healthiest motivation, the longest-lasting motivation, is one of gratitude for God's indwelling presence. In the movie *Chariots of Fire*, Eric Liddell comments, "Where does the strength come from to see the race to its end? It comes from within."

And Jesus says, "the kingdom of God is within you" (Luke 17:21). The kingdom of God is living a life of peace, joy and righteousness in the Holy Spirit (see Romans 14:17).

As Christians, I propose that our X-factor, our courage and our guts come from the presence of the Almighty God in our lives. Not only did Jesus live a perfect life as an example for us to follow, but He also went a step further and gave us His very Spirit to guide and empower us. That's what we celebrate at Christmas: "Emmanuel"—God with us. The mystery of God's presence is made possible by the Third Person in the Godhead, the Holy Spirit.

The original Greek word for Holy Spirit is *paraclete*. That means "advocate" or "comforter who comes alongside." It is a great comfort knowing that God is right alongside us, even inside of us. We

131

need His Spirit to discipline ourselves to push through the hard times. Paul explains in 2 Timothy 1:7, "For God did not give us a spirit of timidity, but a spirit of power, of love and of self-discipline."

Gordon MacDonald says it well:

Discipline is the act of inducing pain and stress in one's life in order to grow into greater toughness, capacity, endurance or strength. So spiritual discipline is that effort of pressing the soul so that it will enlarge its capacity to hear God speak and, as a result, to generate inner force that will guide and empower one's mind and outer life.

True guts come from leaning on the Holy Spirit to guide and empower us to endure and give thanks in all things. Guts come from knowing what you are about and what you stand for, and from remembering who you are, Whose you are and Who's in you! As the saying goes, "No guts, no glory!"

Insights into the Heart of a Champion

Rev. Canon Dr. John Ashley Null
Two-time Olympic Chaplain

To be an Olympic chaplain is to experience first-hand that famous Dickensian paradox. You have the unique opportunity to share the indescribable joy of an athlete who has just fulfilled a lifelong quest to attain the ultimate sporting achievement. You also have the even greater privilege to stand by and support the many more athletes who have just seen their life's dream shattered before their eyes. For in sport, every person's thrill of victory comes at the cost of many, many other people's agony of defeat. That is the nature of competition. Nothing made this harsh reality more clear to me than the USA swim team's Olympic trials for Sydney 2000 in the 200-meters men's freestyle.

The meet was in Indianapolis, and I had flown in to help with the daily swimmers' chapel, a program led by Josh Davis, at his request. I had known Josh since 1991 when we met at the World University Games in Sheffield, England. Back then Josh had just completed his freshman year at the University of Texas and was competing in his first major international competition. I was taking a three-week break from my PhD studies at the University of Cambridge to serve once again as a sports chaplain. We hit it off at once. Josh was eager to learn more about Christ, and it was a joy for me to help him integrate his growing faith with his increasing success in sport. Once the Sheffield Games were over, I promised to continue to support Josh at his major competitions.

By 2000, Josh had become a veteran member of the U.S. National Team with three Olympic gold medals from Atlanta, the

most of any male athlete at those games. Despite his success, however, he had yet to achieve his lifelong goal of breaking the American record in the men's 200-meter freestyle set by his childhood
hero, Matt Biondi.

Josh's roommate in Indy was Ugur Taner. Their stories could
not have been more different. At 13, Josh was told by his coach to
find another sport because he lacked promise. By 14, Ugur had
become the fastest American swimmer ever for his age. In 1992,
Josh watched the Barcelona Games on television. Ugur competed
in them for Turkey.

But in 1996, their roles were reversed. Ugur tried and just
missed making the U.S. team with Josh. This time it was Ugur who
was forced to watch his friends on TV, while Josh went on to
Olympic glory. Four years later, at 26, the 2000 trials were Ugur's
last chance to fulfill all those expectations that came from his incredible success as a high school student—the expectations of his
coaches, of his family and of himself. As Ugur writes in his own
contribution to this book, "Less than 1 percent of all swimmers at
the trials actually make the team, so you can imagine the level of
stress I felt preparing for competition."

As was our usual routine at a major event, I went to Josh's ho-
tel room at 4:00 P.M. to pray with him before the finals in the 200-
meter freestyle event that evening. Six months earlier, Ugur had
become a Christian. I have to say that his decision to follow Jesus
as his Savior and Lord had been a great surprise to everyone. After
all, being Turkish-American, Ugur had a decidedly non-Christian
family background. But Josh was overjoyed to have a fellow born-
again believer on the National Team, even if they were direct competitors in the 200-meter freestyle. So Ugur was invited to join our
prayer session. I prayed with each swimmer individually, and then
we all prayed together. We asked that God would enable both Josh
and Ugur to fulfill their calling and have the peace, power and sense
of God's presence to perform at their very best.

The race was very, very fast and oh so close. In less than two minutes it was all over. Josh had at long last broken the American record. But Ugur had just missed the Olympic team once again—this time by 1/100th of a second. Both felt a degree of emotional intensity that neither had ever known before. For Josh, it was joy and the hope of better things to come. For Ugur, it was the bitter pain of the things deeply hoped for that could now never be.

As chaplain to both men, we three all had dinner together afterward—a simultaneous toasting of Josh's new record and a eulogy for Ugur's long-held athletic dream. It was surreal. Josh tried desperately to be sensitive to Ugur. Ugur tried desperately to be happy for Josh. I tried desperately to help both sense God's presence with them at this equally momentous but vastly different moment in their lives. Sitting at that table, I was confronted with hope and heartache, cheek by jowl, the epitome of life as an Olympic chaplain.

What do you say? How do you explain such a turn of events? Was 2/100ths of a second too much to ask from God Almighty? Did the Heavenly Watchman who promises neither to slumber nor sleep for a mere instant blink? Did God just love Josh more? Or was Ugur such a big sinner that he didn't deserve to make the team?

Such questions may sound stupid, but not if you have been there. When the sting of defeat is still white hot, the human heart cries out for answers. And even years later, when a person least expects it, something can trigger that old memory. Then, with breathtaking speed, the pain rushes back in a moment and the hunger for an explanation roars back to life all over again. All the while, the enemy of our soul is right there spinning out his suggestions, offering his lies as a solution, seeking to take our pain and only deepen it by turning our hearts against our heavenly Father who allowed us to experience such devastating disappointment.

In such moments, it is all too easy for Christian athletes to see God as their ultimate coach. Those who feel they have made good spiritual choices often expect to be included on God's winning team and be blessed with athletic success. Those who have made bad choices can easily fear that they will be left off the roster and cut out of any reward—at least until they can prove themselves to be better spiritually again. When Christian athletes lose, they cannot help but wonder what failure of regular Christian duty, what recent bad moral choice, or even what ongoing inner unworthiness made God decide that they were not good enough to have their best efforts blessed with success. As a result, in the very moment these athletes need help from their relationship with God the most, their faith can easily become just another reason to feel ashamed for being a loser. In the final analysis, the only thing worse than feeling that you let down your country, your coach, your teammates, your family, your friends and yourself is thinking the reason for all this pain is that you let down God, too.

Even winning is not without its emotional sand traps. After years spent dreaming of how wonderful an Olympic victory is going to be, the thrill—as incredible as it is—fades so very quickly. The next morning comes, like every new morning, with its own fresh set of problems. Athletic success doesn't insulate you from all the stresses and strains of normal life. Indeed, with the special status of being a world champion comes a whole new set of special problems: Who are my real friends? Does that person care about me or just want to brag about knowing an Olympic gold medalist? How come everybody always expects something from me? How do I squeeze in all these appearances for my new sponsors while still train to stay on top? Isn't there any time anymore just for me? What if I lose? How long can I ride this wave? What happens to me when my body gives out and it's all over?

The heart of an Olympic chaplain must understand the heart of all those who long to become champions when they achieve their goals and when they do not. In the face of all of the intense aspirations and anxieties that elite sports people encounter, chaplains must be convincing witnesses to the truth of God's enduring unconditional love and the power of his promises to deliver a peace and purpose that passes all human understanding. After all, that's why a chaplain is given access to the athletic holy of holies, the Olympic Village: to be at the side of those competitors who wish to turn to God in preparation for their events and then to help them make spiritual sense of the results afterward. Clearly, it's not an easy task.

To fulfill these daunting responsibilities, chaplains must first learn to look beyond all the glitter of the Games. Hard-core fans enjoy watching the Olympics because they identify with their heroes' successes. They escape from the tensions of everyday living by daydreaming of how wonderful it must be to live the life of an Olympian. Caught up in all the global glamour and excitement, such fans cannot begin to imagine the immense strain that so many of the competitors feel 24/7 in the Village. They don't even try. After all, who includes pressures and problems in their fantasies? Consequently, fans do not make good chaplains.

Being in the Village—the very heart of the whole Games—wearing an official Olympic uniform, trading delegation pins with other participants, meeting athletes from around the world, perhaps being introduced to somebody famous and maybe even getting complimentary tickets to an Olympic event such as the open or closing ceremonies . . . are all too much of a distraction for fans who want to serve as chaplains. Having a once-in-a-lifetime chance really to live out their fantasy of an Olympic lifestyle, they remain completely blind to the struggles of the athletes they are there to serve. *After all,* they think, *it's so great to be taking part in the Games. How can Olympians have any real problems?* And if you can't see their problems, you can't be part of the solution.

The great irony is that Olympic athletes can spot such "sports groupies" a mile away and will avoid them at all cost. By the end of the Games, fans who manage to become chaplains can easily wind up all alone in the religious services center. And there are few feelings worse than being at the heart of an event watched by more than two billion people from around the world while nobody there even notices that you exist. Like so many of the athletes around them, fans who push their way in to serve as chaplains often find that their Olympic dream has turned out to be a heartache.

Thus, true sports chaplains have to understand not only the heart of elite athletes but also their own hearts. They have to be willing to stop and assess their motives afresh each and every day. Are they acting like mere fans masquerading as pastors? Or, even worse, are they using their insider's knowledge of the problems faced by Olympians to advance their own personal or professional agenda? Are they in fact just being users like everyone else that hangs around celebrities?

Facing yourself is always difficult, but it is especially hard for those who minister to the sporting elite. On the surface, their motivation is clear—to advance the cause of Christ. But, as Scripture warns us, "The heart is deceitful above all things and beyond cure. Who can understand it?" (Jeremiah 17:9). Self-centered human nature dies hard, even for mature Christians. Olympic chaplains are no exception, and they have so many ways to stumble!

Are the chaplains former athletes who never fulfilled their own sporting ambitions? Then they can easily see mentoring high-profile athletes as a God-ordained redemption of their own dream to be part of that elite crowd. Are the chaplains former Olympians themselves? Then they can simply be trying to relive the glory moments of their ever-fading fame and physical prowess. Are the chaplains committed to world evangelism? Then they can easily be seeking to get close to champions, because through a sports star's platform, their own ministry will end up influencing tens of thousands of more people than the chaplains could ever do directly themselves. Are the chaplains full-time Christian workers needing to raise their own support? Then there are few better ways for them to gain credibility with potential donors than by being able to say that they are Olympic chaplains. Indeed, perhaps the most effective fundraising technique is for chaplains to seek to mentor an Olympic gold medalist at the Games so that they can then ask the champion to testify publicly how important their role was in his or her achievement.

The honest truth is that the enemy of our soul is an equal-opportunity deceiver. Every morning brings new chances for chaplains to forget that their role is all about the athletes, not about themselves. Ministering at the highest levels of worldly society, experienced Olympic chaplains, like mature Christian Olympians, struggle with mixed motivations.

Therefore, the heart of a seasoned sports chaplain must also understand the heart of Jesus—this is the final and most important key to an effective ministry. Chaplains must know that it is the Lord's joy not only to *save* His people by grace but also to *sustain* them by His grace. That means that experienced chaplains find their continuing self-esteem not in their constant sweat in Jesus' service but because of the ongoing redemptive effects of Christ's sacrifice on the cross for them. It is for this reason alone that chaplains can be confident of their calling in the Olympic world despite their clear and ever-present shortcomings. For God Almighty is faithful to bring forth good fruit from even their faltering efforts. Once the Holy Spirit has written this truth on their hearts, seasoned chaplains can begin to break free from that fundamental untruth of the sports world that warps everyone associated with it—that a person's value is based solely on his or her current performance. By leaning on God's grace to walk in freedom from this lie, Olympic chaplains experience the divinely given comfort with which they can comfort the athletes to whom they minister (see 2 Corinthians 1:3-5).

When chaplains express in their own conduct a trust in God's prodigal love and providential care, their personal faith becomes contagious. As Olympic athletes encounter such living witnesses to the power of God's promises, they too begin to trust God not only for their sins but also for their athletic dreams. Gradually, they learn that the value of all their struggle, sweat and self-investment in sport is ultimately not determined by the scoreboard but by God's faithfulness to use everything for His eternal purposes. Whether they set a new record or miss the Olympic team by 1/100th of a second, they find lasting peace in God's plan for their life.

Does that sound too good to be true? Here's the truth: In the Christian life, God takes each of us on journeys that we do not wish to go. He makes us travel by roads we do not wish to use. He does all this so that He can bring us to places we never wish to leave. That is the nature of our Lord's unchanging, unconditional love for each one of us. Nothing has made this hopeful reality more clear to me than watching God's pastoral care of Josh and Ugur since the trials.

In 2004, Josh himself tasted the bitter disappointment of not qualifying for another Olympics. He would eventually retire to concentrate on his great love—motivating people to dream great dreams and achieve their best. Today, Josh speaks on average to 500 youths and adults every week all around the country. This book is just one of numerous examples by which Josh wishes to encourage people to hear God's calling on their lives and to embrace fully the journey the heavenly Father has planned for them.

And Ugur? Faced with the death of his life-long ambition so shortly after he became a Christian, Ugur had to wrestle deep in his soul with why he had turned away from his family background to come to Jesus. Had he in reality just tried to take out an insurance policy? Was he merely hoping to get the Christian God on his side so that he would surely win his place on the Olympic team, like Josh? If so, now was the time to admit his mistake, move on and move away from the Christian lies he had so foolishly listened to. Or were the claims of Christ true? Was Jesus' love in his heart more than enough to make life worth living, regardless of his loss? If so, now Ugur needed to lean on the grace of God to sustain him through all his doubts and despair until God made clear to him a new, deeply satisfying direction for his future.

Ugur discovered that Jesus' love would not let him go! Despite the ups and downs of coming to terms with the end of his sporting career, Ugur found his trust, hope, love and, yes, even gratitude toward his Savior growing little by little with every passing day. And Ugur was not the only person to notice the deepening, maturing faith at work in him. Liesl, his not-yet Christian wife, was too close not to see the changes—the wonderful changes—happening to this man she loved so much. She had wanted nothing else but to heal her husband's broken heart, but her own heart broke when she discovered she couldn't. Then, when she saw Jesus doing for her husband what she longed to see, she found herself slowly falling in love with a Savior who so clearly loved her husband as deeply as she did. Four years later, Ugur's long-standing prayers were answered. Liesl became a Christian, and together they began to build a new family heritage—a Christian heritage—that today they share with three wonderful children. Six years after the trials, Ugur left his job at a large swim school in California to follow a new calling as the audio-visual director at his local church. Today, his life continues to center around the joy of serving God, not because God made his Olympic dreams come true, but because God gave him an even better dream for his family and made it come to pass in an unexpected but fully effective way.

How about you? Have you seen God's always-challenging but ever-faithful pastoral care at work in your life? Have you learned to lean on His grace so that you can trust that His love will eventually take you to places you never wish to leave?

SECTION
THREE

GLORY

Krystal Thomas

Leah O'Brien-Amico

Jennie Finch

Eric Liddell

Cat Reddick Whitehill

Amanda Borden

Introduction

There is something special about the Olympic Games. Every four years, we see a glimpse of human greatness, and it inspires us to become something more. These visual images of glory are forever etched in our minds. Berlin 1936: Jesse Owens wins four gold medals as Adolph Hitler looks on. Los Angeles 1984: Mary Lou Retton, with her gold-medal smile, scores a perfect 10 on the vault exercise. Atlanta 1996: Wearing his "gold" shoes in front of a home crowd, Michael Johnson crushes the world record in the 200-meter. Sydney 2000: My teammates Gary Hall, Jr. and Anthony Ervin tie for first in swimming's premiere event, the 50-meter freestyle. Athens 2004: The 4x200-meter freestyle relay team of Michael Phelps, Ryan Lochte, Peter Vanderkay and Klete Keller touch out the Australians, whom they hadn't beaten in 7 years. I could watch these highlights every day! (Secret confession: I do!)

But what makes these moments so full of "glory"? They are characterized by beauty, exceptional skill and a degree of excellence seldom encountered this side of heaven. When an athlete overcomes insurmountable odds, we call it a "glorious comeback." When an athlete nails the perfect routine, run, swim or shot, we call it a "moment of glory." These moments are special because they help us see that the impossible is not only possible, but achievable.

Many of the following stories contain moments of physical glory, moments when world-class athletes flawlessly executed their rare talents. However, these stories also illustrate a *spiritual* glory that transcends mere competition. The real "miracle" of athletic competition lies in adopting an attitude that reflects the character of God, while taking actions that glorify Him. In 2 Corinthians 3:18, Paul says that just as Moses reflected God's glory, how much more "we, who with unveiled faces all reflect the Lord's glory, are being transformed into his likeness with ever-increasing glory, which comes from the Lord, who is the Spirit."

It is truly a glorious moment when God takes a selfish, sin-filled heart and changes it so much that we not only conform to His will, but also embrace it. We reflect a heart like His, a heart that loves! The ultimate glory is found when God transforms our hearts into mirrors of His love to the world.

Is it possible to achieve personal glory as well as God's glory? After reading these incredible stories, I think you will discover for yourself that we serve a big God and that what is impossible for man is always possible for God. So, while these athletes may receive personal glory on the medal stand, the ultimate recipient of all adoration and glory is God alone.

1

Fleeting Highs and Lasting Joys

Josh Davis
Three-time U.S. Olympic Gold Medalist in Swimming

*We long to hold on to timeless moments here on Earth, but they
slip away like sand through our fingers. This is evidence that we were
created for an existence where those moments never end.
God truly has written eternity in our hearts.*

JOSH DAVIS

At the 1996 Atlanta Olympic Games, as I stared down my lane to
lead off the U.S. 4x200 freestyle relay, the thought crossed my
mind that 4 hours of swimming each day for 10 years—a total of
25,000 miles—now came down to one moment in time. On top of
all that, for the first time ever in history, our relay team was the
underdog, predicted by the experts to *maybe* get third-place bronze.
After a stinging disappointment in my individual 200-meter freestyle the night before, I was determined not to let the overwhelming pressure hinder me. I was confident that I could do better.

With added motivation from the guys, my focus and adrenaline had never been higher. The starter's gun released me, and I
led off the relay with a lifetime best! My early lead got the rest of
the team pumped up even more. In the end, my teammates Joe
Hudepohl, Brad Schumacker and Ryan Berube also shared lifetime bests, thus lengthening our lead—amazingly, we won by over
a body length! The joy and relief we felt was indescribable. The in-

tense satisfaction of accomplishing a lifelong dream in front of a home crowd and of coming together with my relay mates in perfect execution was a high I had never felt before. I was smiling so big my face began to get sore.

Soon after, we put the red, white and blue awards jacket on, and were escorted to the three-tiered podium for the medal ceremony. As they announced, "Gold Medal, United States of America," we all stood up together waving to the 10,000 screaming fans. I couldn't believe it was happening! I finally was the best, the very best! To be on the award stand with the crowd on its feet for us, to see our flag raised, to hear our beautiful national anthem played and to finally feel the weight of the gold medal hang around my neck . . . in a word, it was awesome!

The next several hours were a blur of high-fives, hugs and hellos. The elation of celebrating with family and teammates was incredible. We walked with our heads high—we knew we had made everybody in the United States proud. Soon, we were whisked off to a live interview for NBC, while *ESPN* and *Sports Illustrated* wanted some memorable quotes. Everybody we saw treated us like gods. I finally fell asleep that night with my new gold medal around my neck and that same huge smile on my face.

When I woke up the next morning, all the excitement, all the hype, all the adrenaline . . . it was all gone! Granted, I was still living in the Olympic Village, eating the free food and looking forward to some more races, but the mood was so drastically different from the night before.

I had finally tasted the best the world had to offer and it was sweet . . . but oh, so short! Having had a taste of glory, I now felt empty. It was sobering to experience the shock of a high so high followed by a low so low. I was a little confused and disillusioned.

In that moment, I knew where to look to find encouragement and perspective: God's Word. When I opened my Bible, it fell open to 1 Peter 1:7: "Your faith . . . [is] of greater worth than gold." I found comfort in the knowledge that my relationship with Jesus is infinitely more valuable and more precious than gold.

Next, I came across Matthew 6:19-21: "Do not store up for yourselves treasures on earth, where moth and rust destroy, and where thieves break in and steal. But store up for yourselves treasures in heaven, where moth and rust do not destroy, and where thieves do not break in and steal. For where your treasure is, there your heart will be also." I realized then that my medal wouldn't last forever, but it was good to know that there is something that will.

When I give motivational speeches at schools, I routinely pass my gold medal around the room so that each student can hold it or wear it. I always enjoy watching the reactions of the children: Their eyes get big as they "ooh" and "ahh." Several people over the years have accidentally dropped my medal, and it is dented and scratched. And it's not just my medal that shows some wear. My cool monogrammed Olympic suitcase is falling apart, my Olympic towels are starting to unravel and some of my Olympic clothes have bleach stains.

This wear and tear reminds me that, eventually, everything material in this world will fall apart. God's Word reminds us that there are only three eternal things: God, His Word, and the souls of men and women. And when we invest our lives accordingly, by serving God and others in and through His love, we are storing up gold medals in heaven that will last forever.

Yes, I still smile when I watch the tape of my team winning—but not as much as I do when I discover someone has committed his or her life to Christ! While only a few know what it's like to win a medal at the Games, the experience will pale in comparison to the awards ceremony we will have in heaven. If you train your heart while you train your body, you too will have the lasting joy of being a gold-medal winner in Christ!

Is your faith in Christ and relationship with Him the most important treasure in your life? How can you train for the temporal while investing in the eternal? How can you train with all your heart to win the race over others but stay focused on the well-being of the souls of others? In your daily routine as a parent, businessperson or sports champion, spend time memorizing God's Word. Spend time talking to God. And spend time loving, feeding and caring for others.

Therefore we do not lose heart. Though outwardly we are wasting away, yet inwardly we are being renewed day by day. For our light and momentary troubles are achieving for us an eternal glory that far outweighs them all. So we fix our eyes not on what is seen, but on what is unseen. For what is seen is temporary, but what is unseen is eternal.

2 Corinthians 4:16-18

2

No Substitutions Allowed

Annett Davis
U.S. Olympic Beach Volleyball Team

Anything less than a conscious commitment to the important is
an unconscious commitment to the unimportant.
STEPHEN COVEY

When I eat my meals, I like certain things. I enjoy ketchup on my eggs and parmesan reggiano cheese on my pasta. Any day, I prefer spaghetti to fettuccine or linguine, and hash browns to potatoes.

One day at a restaurant, I considered switching some things in my order I didn't like until I noticed in bold print, "No Substitutions Allowed."

At this particular eating establishment, you couldn't add or subtract from their exact menu. The master chef had invested hours creating, adjusting and tasting his menu dishes until they were perfect. With his years of training, numerous awards and impeccable palate, he knew what his meals were supposed to taste like. Any substitutions would be considered an insult.

Likewise, we serve a God who is the Master of the universe. He created all and designed everything to work according to His marvelous plan. There is nothing better, no other combination that would make more sense. His ways are the best ways; His plans for us are perfect. In our relationship with Him, He desires us to seek Him first, to follow Him daily, and He never wants substitutions to take His place in our lives.

Admittedly, sometimes I still unintentionally try to substitute television, the Internet, friends and family, or recreation for time with God.

What are your substitutes?

O God, you are my God, earnestly I seek you; my soul thirsts for you, my body longs for you, in a dry and weary land where there is no water. My soul will be satisfied as with the richest of foods; with singing lips my mouth will praise you.

PSALM 63:1,5

Standing Still When Life Says, "Run!"

Allyson Felix
U.S. Olympic Silver Medalist in Track and Field

I believe God made me for a purpose, but he also made me fast.
And when I run I feel His pleasure.
ERIC LIDDELL

Growing up in Southern California, I wanted to be just like my older brother. He ran track, so I decided to try out for the track team during my freshman year at Los Angeles Baptist High School. During tryouts, my times were so fast that I remember the coach doing a doubletake to make sure he had read his stopwatch correctly.

In my best event, the 200-meter sprint, I went on to win several state high school championships and become the fastest high school female athlete ever. I began to compete not only for high school titles, but also for World Championship and Olympic titles as well.

I reached the highest level of athletic success at a young age, and that was all very exciting and gratifying. But a nagging injury during my junior year of high school caused me to seriously question my future in track and field. I was expected to win big at the World Juniors in Jamaica that year, but a hamstring injury slowed me down and I placed a disappointing fifth place in the 200-meter sprint. Newspaper articles said that I had "choked."

Like many athletes who face failure, I considered quitting. To find encouragement and peace, I opened up God's Word.

There are a lot of great verses in the Bible about running. In the book of Hebrews, we are challenged to "run with perseverance the race marked out for us" (12:1). We are also encouraged to "run in such a way as to get the prize" (1 Corinthians 9:24). These and other verses have definitely encouraged me as I strive to live my life in a Christlike manner.

The idea of running comes naturally to me. "Standing still" and just trusting in God is harder for me. But in Exodus 14:13, God calls us to do just that: "Stand still, and see the salvation of the Lord" (NKJV). As I started to feel sorry for myself and looked to do something in my own power, God gently brought me back to a place of "stillness" and reminded me that He is in control, He is faithful, and that He is the only One who brings complete fulfillment to my life . . . not athletics.

Winning the silver medal in the 200-meter dash at the 2004 Athens Olympic Games was the most exhilarating moment of my life. And as I stood on that medal stand as the youngest member of the U.S. track and field team, I felt a tremendous sense of both pride and humility.

During the Games, I relied on the challenge the apostle Paul gave to Timothy: "Do not let anyone look down on you because you are young." Among veteran teammates and more experienced opponents, I held fast to this truth to calm my anxious heart. And you know what? God's unceasing love and faithfulness gave me the peace to do my best!

Are you attempting to run away from the place God has called you to? Do you feel inadequate or too young for the task God is calling you to accomplish? My prayer is that you will "stand still" today and experience the joy of an intimate relationship with Jesus Christ.

Stand still, and see the salvation of the Lord.
EXODUS 14:13, *NKJV*

Suspended in Your Presence

Madeline Manning Mims
U.S. Olympic Gold Medalist in Track

You will never go where God is not. You may be transferred, enlisted, commissioned, reassigned, or hospitalized, but—brand this truth on your heart—you can never go where God is not.

MAX LUCADO

We are always *in* God's Presence, but not always *aware* of His Presence. I love to feel Him so near that He becomes the very air I breathe. I wrote a song to that effect.

Suspended in Your Presence

Suspended in Your Presence, surrounded by Your peace,
Wrapped up in Your affections, secured in sweet release.

I'm raptured in Your glory, held captive by Your grace.
You breathe Your breath into me, my heart pulsates with faith.

You're the Alpha, You're the Omega, the God who cannot lie.
Your promises never fail me, You're the river that won't run dry.

And I know Your voice within me, Yes I know I am Your bride.
Your sweet love never fails me, Your Presence gives me life.

Oh, the glory of Your Presence! I am suspended in time
When I am Yours and You're mine.

Oh how my heart overflows, when in Your Presence I know
That I am suspended in Your love, touched from above,
Safe in the arms of my God.
Always, forever, I'm in Your Presence.[1]

Do you want to feel His presence? Then pray:

*Father, I want to be more sensitive to Your Presence in every area
of my life. To know You are there is self-control. You have said,
"My peace I leave with you." You are my peace in Christ Jesus, and I can
do all things through the sufficiency of Christ. Amen.*

Trust that God is present and working behind the scenes for
you, even when you can't feel His presence.

*You will show me the path of life: in Your Presence is fullness of joy;
at Your right hand are pleasures forevermore.*
PSALM 16:11, *NKJV*

Note
1. "Suspended in Your Presence," © 1999 Madeline Manning Mims.

5

Eternal Investment

John Register
U.S. Hurdles/Swimming Paralympian

I have made it a goal to live a life worth contemplating throughout eternity, a life lived without regrets, not squandered, but lived for Christ.
CONGRESSMAN JIM RYUN

The apostle Paul teaches that making a difference for Christ in other peoples' lives glorifies our heavenly Father and signifies that we are Jesus' disciples (see John 15:8).

Years ago, as this truth of John 15:8 really sunk in, I questioned if my life was *really* making an eternal difference. For three years I kept asking God, "Where is my fruit for You?" Each time, I seemed to get a confirmation through a sermon or Bible passage that my life was having an impact, even if I couldn't see it yet.

One day, completely out of the blue, I received Army orders to go to Operation Desert Shield/Desert Storm. I was totally floored. First of all, I was in non-deployment status. Second, I was under orders to transfer to San Francisco. Third, I had already started leadership training. Any one of those things should have stopped my deployment, but none did.

Not looking forward to 125 degrees in the shade, I earnestly asked God, "Why?"

Gently, God whispered to my soul, "This is the opportunity you've been asking for. You're going to see your fruit."

That gave me peace about going.

On the bus ride to the plane, I sat next to a Hispanic kid. We began talking and I ended up sharing about my faith in Jesus. After our brief 20-minute conversation, I didn't see him again.

At our camp overseas, the commander let us set up a little tent to conduct a Bible study. Within a few days, 35 to 40 people were attending every night. We'd read through the Bible together, and I'd give a little message. Watching people openly share their requests and come to faith in Christ excited me.

After a temporary guard duty assignment away from our camp, I was surprised upon my return to discover our little Bible study had grown to 110 people. My second night back, I couldn't believe my eyes. The same Hispanic kid that I had met two months earlier was taking part! At the end of the study, he came forward and surrendered his life to Christ.

As an athlete I've known the sweet taste of victory, but I can tell you nothing is as sweet as seeing the victory of Jesus written on the face of a fresh believer. As this young man shared his journey to faith, he pointed right at me and said, "It's because of him that Jesus is my Lord."

He shared how I had planted the seed of the hope of the gospel in his heart on that bus ride and how God had used others to water and nurture it. I had only been one of many. Yet that night, God gave me the gift of seeing how He could use me to make a difference.

Twenty minutes of my time on the bus and now that young man will spend eternity in heaven. Talk about a faith booster!

Never doubt God's ability to use your availability to make an eternal difference.

Make the most of your chances to tell others the Good News.
Be wise in all your contacts with them.
COLOSSIANS 4:5, *TLB*

6

Giving My All for the Almighty

Josh Davis
Three-time U.S. Olympic Gold Medalist in Swimming

Success is peace of mind which is a direct result of
self-satisfaction in knowing you made the effort to become
the best you are capable of becoming.
JOHN WOODEN

The Sydney race was the biggest in my life—the fastest ever Olympic final of my favorite event, the 200-meter freestyle! All of my years of training culminated in just 1 minute and 46 seconds!

As I prepared for the race, you can imagine the intensity of emotion I felt as so many thoughts ran through my mind. I asked God for His grace, wisdom and strength. Purposefully, I gave my doubts, fears and worries to Him, and renewed my mind with God's truth, thanks to the encouragement of my Olympic chaplain and friend, Dr. Ashley Null.

As the eight of us finalists gathered in the ready room, we knew it would be a four-man race: Ian, the Aussie who was favored to win; Peter, the flying Dutchman; Massi, the fast Italian; and me, the lone American. We were four of the best swimmers in the world, competing for three medals. We looked at each other, knowing that one of us would not get a medal.

As we filed into the darkened hallway before marching onto the brightly lit pool deck, all I could see were the huge shoulders of Ian in front of me. At 6' 5" and 220 pounds, Ian, who hadn't been beaten in years, was an intimidating opponent. The two-minute wait to march out seemed more like two hours. I quickly prayed against thoughts of fear, resting in God's provision. Just as He had so many times before, I knew that He would give me what I needed when I needed it, and not a second too soon.

The inescapable moment arrived: The monotone voice echoed throughout the venue, "Please welcome the finalists in the men's 200-meter freestyle." As we walked out from under the awning, a wave of lights and noise from the 18,000 cheering fans greeted us. The deafening crowd had been anticipating this race for days, and I couldn't help but smile and embrace that amazing moment.

Right before the race, the official called us to the blocks, and I said one last prayer: "Lord, help me go all out for You and with You, regardless of my time or place. Thank You for being with me. Let's have some fun!" In just a few seconds, the amazingly loud crowd came to a complete silence. As the announcer instructed, "Swimmers, take your mark," I thought of the 25,000 miles of training that had led to this moment.

Bang! The starter's gun released me into the water to race just 200 meters. I felt great and touched ahead in a world-record pace on the first turn at the 50-meter mark. By halfway at the 100-meter turn, Peter, Ian and I were right together and Massi the Italian was a meter behind us. On the last turn at the 150-meter mark, Peter and Ian were tied for first, I was right behind them and the Italian was still a meter behind me. With one lap to go, I was in a solid third, and if I held that spot, I would win the bronze medal!

All of a sudden, Massi caught up with me and he and I were neck and neck, stroke for stroke. In the final meters, we put our heads down and reached for the wall. I looked up at the scoreboard and saw the number 4 next to my name. Peter had won, with Ian second, and Massi had touched me out for third place. My heart sank.

At the Games, they say that fourth place is the worst place to be—whether you place last or fourth, you don't receive a medal. But I looked at my time and saw that I had swum 1:46:7! That time broke my own American record by a good margin and would have easily won at the previous Olympic Games.

In that moment, I realized that my prayer had been answered! God had been with me during the race so that I could swim my best, and He was with me now! God had been glorified, and I had swum faster than ever before. I was part of the fastest 200-meter freestyle race of all time.

Even though I was pleased with my time, after an Olympic final there is a tremendous amount of emotion. I was overwhelmed with disappointment for missing a medal by seven one-hundredths of a second. I had trained so hard for so long, and to miss my goal by such a small margin stung bitterly. To be honest, I cried. I could not separate my emotions from the reality of having sacrificed so much.

But that's the beauty of having a genuine relationship with God. We can be totally human, vulnerable, honest and real. Although my feelings didn't line up with God's truth at that moment, I still trusted Him and experienced His joy, deep down. Happiness comes and goes—as does intense sadness—but real joy is always there, regardless of the circumstances. I found comfort and strength in remembering that God loves me unconditionally—and that He was proud of me for my dependence on Him and sacrifice to Him.

It's tough when you come from a country where winning is everything. In our cultural economy, performance determines worth, but in God's economy, Christ's performance determines value. I learned that no win, no medal, will make Jesus love me any more than He did when He died on the cross, even as I was rejecting Him. Jesus' unconditional and unwavering love for me freed me from any lingering doubts about my own worth, even when I wasn't No. 1 in the eyes of the world.

God calls each of us to set ourselves apart, giving our all, acknowledging His presence and relying on His power and peace. He wants us to give our best to His glory!

Ask God to free you to enjoy life, regardless of your position or status. May you never doubt that you are always loved!

And this is my prayer: that your love may abound more and more in knowledge and depth of insight, so that you may be able to discern what is best and may be pure and blameless until the day of Christ.
PHILIPPIANS 1:9-10

7

Climbing Higher

Laura Wilkinson
U.S. Olympic Gold Medalist in Diving

*True success is knowing your worth in the eyes of God,
and using your gifts properly.*
FRANKLIN JENTEZEN

Six months before the 2000 Sydney Olympics, I injured my foot during a routine warm-up at a meet in Florida. The doctor in the emergency room dismissed me with a pair of crutches without taking X-rays.

I returned home five days later still in extreme pain, so my mom took me to my doctor for a second opinion. My doctor was distraught when she saw the X-rays, which showed three broken bones that could have been initially reset. However, after just those first few days, my bones had already begun to heal incorrectly.

Leaving the doctor's office with the first of three different casts, I felt my Olympic dreams slipping away. I was angry and depressed. Although I was relieved that the pressure to make the 2000 U.S. Olympic team was gone, I was upset that I couldn't dive. In the midst of my gamut of emotions, Kenny, my coach, came to my apartment and abruptly ended my pity party. Together we decided that my dream was still worth pursuing.

With a cast on my foot for 10 weeks, I couldn't train like I normally did: 6 days a week for 6 hours a day. Instead, Kenny had me climb up to the 10-meter platform and go through the motions of my dives while also visualizing them in my head.

So every day, I hopped on my crutches from my apartment, across the street to the pool, and climbed up to the platform and pretended to do my dives. Sometimes I felt silly up there pretending to do something I couldn't, but my teammates encouraged me and cheered me on every time they saw me struggle.

Just three weeks before the 2000 Olympic trials, I was able to start diving again. Despite my limitations, I miraculously made the team. But a greater challenge still awaited: China had captured the gold in the last four Olympics, and I had to face them in Sydney.

I like to recite Philippians 4:13 before I dive. During the Games in Sydney, this verse especially encouraged me to endure the intense pain from my foot injury. Remembering that Christ is the source of my strength made me feel like I could overcome anything, even diving against the odds and trying to win a medal.

The moment that stands out the most to me from the Olympics happened right before my final dive. I didn't know what my score was; I just knew I was in the running for a medal. I realized at that moment that I was living out my dream. I didn't even care what the outcome would be—if I won or not. I gave glory to God in that moment and captured it like a panoramic picture etched in my mind.

I nailed that dive, winning the gold! Despite the media frenzy about my "underdog" victory, there was no doubt in my mind that all things are possible with God.

When we experience disappointment and brokenness in our lives, God gives us an extraordinary ability to step up and accomplish amazing things as we rely on His strength. Do you see your present difficulties as an opportunity for God to demonstrate His power and glory?

That is why, for Christ's sake, I delight in weaknesses, in insults, in hardships, in persecutions, in difficulties. For when I am weak, then I am strong.
2 CORINTHIANS 12:10

8

Coming Up for Air

Brooke Abel
U.S. Olympic Synchronized Swimming

Take rest; a field that has rested gives a bountiful crop.
OVID

Drowning is not typically something people do on purpose. Yet in my sport, I feel close to drowning every day. Our routines usually last about four minutes, and within those four minutes we get very few opportunities to come up for air. It is essential that our team memorizes our programs flawlessly because we can't afford to miss our chance to breathe. If we do, everything ends—without air, we can't keep performing.

If God is the air we breathe, like the popular worship song proclaims, how can we live without daily inhaling God's love and exhaling the stress that weighs us down? Theologian Charles Spurgeon wrote, "I earnestly wish that many who have never felt that rest, would come and have it . . . if God enables them to exercise a simple act of faith in Jesus, he will give them . . . a rest which shall be his glory and to their joy."

Are you desperate for God to breathe life back into you? Have you come to Jesus, who gives perfect rest?

Are you tired? Worn out? I'll show you how to take a real rest.
MATTHEW 11:28-29, *THE MESSAGE*

9

For His Glory

Congressman Jim Ryun
U.S. Olympic Silver Medalist in the 1500-Meter Run

*Some people give time, some give money, some their skills
and connections. Some literally give their life's blood.
But everyone has something to give.*

BARBARA BUSH

People often think that my running career brought me a great deal
of financial gain. Sorry to say, it did not. Strict regulations governing amateur track and field athletes forced me to return many
prizes I won. I couldn't even take home money from speaking en-
gagements. The six-figure appearance fees that top runners com-
mand today were unheard of at the time. Once I turned pro, I did
make good money and hung up my spikes with some savings in
the bank—but I was by no means wealthy.

When I retired from track and field, my fourth child, Catharine, had just been born. I earned my living as a photojournalist,
and money was tight. But my wife, Anne, and I had committed our
lives to Christ several years earlier, so we trusted Him to provide.

During that time in our lives, it was such a struggle to make
ends meet. I clearly remember a group of young Christians who
delivered groceries to our doorstep almost every day. They always
delivered broccoli, and I remember having broccoli for lunch and
dinner: broccoli with butter, broccoli soup, steamed broccoli—any
way you can imagine broccoli being eaten, we ate it.

One morning during that time, I was reading my Bible and praying with Anne. We read Luke 18, the wonderful passage that recounts the time when Jesus told the rich young ruler to give away all he had so that he could follow Him. The young man walked away in sorrow because he was very wealthy and did not want to give up what he owned.

As Anne and I prayed that morning, we both felt strongly that we were to give away our last $100 to our local church. My initial reaction was something like this: *Lord, that's my last $100 right now, and we're having a tough time making ends meet!* I admit I was anxious. Nonetheless, Anne and I couldn't shake the conviction, so we quickly wrote out a check and sent it before our doubts overcame our faith.

I have never regretted the decision, and we were never in want. Scripture assures us, "I [David] have never seen the righteous forsaken or their children begging bread" (Psalm 37:25).

Some people think that once they have tithed, they do not need to consult with God when it comes to the rest of their finances. Not so. We gave away the little money we had at the time, but it was God's anyway. It was a simple decision to make because all that we have is His and should be used for His glory.

To this day, Anne and I make a practice of giving as God directs us to give, and we have taught our children to do the same. I truly believe that everything we possess—talent, money, time, influence, and even broccoli—is God's. It takes spiritual courage, but we must ask ourselves constantly, "How can I use what has been given to me for His glory?"

What talents, time, possessions and influence has God given to you? What is He asking you to invest today—for His glory?

Each man should give what he has decided in his heart to give,
not reluctantly or under compulsion, for God loves a cheerful giver.
2 CORINTHIANS 9:7

10

Never Stop Believing

Shantel Davis
University of Texas Volleyball Team

God's love takes us on journeys we do not wish to go; makes us travel by roads we do not wish to use; to take us to places we never wish to leave.
JOHN ASHLEY NULL

The crowd, colors, flags and sounds were exactly what I'd always dreamed. Suddenly, as if instinctively, the crowd hushed. Within seconds, the welcoming trumpets began to blare. Tears began to roll down my face. I was really there—the 1996 Olympic Games in Atlanta. The only thing wrong with this dream come true was that I was sitting in the stands as a spectator and not marching in the procession as an athlete. My heart broke.

My momentary sadness turned into joy as my husband, Josh Davis, became the only man to win three gold medals at the Games. Riding the wave of excitement, I returned that fall to start my last volleyball season at the University of Texas. My junior year we finished second in the country, so a national title seemed within reach. Unfortunately, the first few weeks into the semester, I injured my back and sat on the bench most of the season. Frustrated, I asked God, "Why did You give me these gifts of leadership and athleticism and not let me use them?" God, in His providence, chose to stay silent.

My hopes of continuing my career faded as we lost in the playoffs, and I became pregnant with our first child three weeks later.

I sought God for new direction and spent months grieving the death of my volleyball dream.

During the following three years, I birthed two more babies as Josh trained to compete in his second Olympic Games. Ultimately, we had five children in eight years and Josh won five Olympic medals.

Eight years later, God responded to my lingering, unanswered question. After a very long day, I felt Him whisper to my heart, "Shantel, now do you understand?"

It had been during my senior year, sitting on the bench, that God had introduced me to the character of Christ. I wrestled with God to accept the truth, for myself, that *every* member of the team has value, not just the one in the spotlight. God forced me to see that great leaders *can* follow if it brings strength to the team.

I had asked, "How?"

He said, "By seeing others as greater than you see yourself."

He pushed me to pursue excellence *without* the roar and applause of the crowd, reassuring me that He was watching, asking me to give my best so that someone else could shine. Then, after stripping me of all my titles, He proclaimed, "You *still* have value!"

All those lessons prepared me to embrace God's beautiful dream for my life: I am a stay-at-home mother of five children, a behind-the-scenes businesswoman, and the wife of a wonderful "spotlight" man. Isn't God gracious?

In trusting Him, I have five "gold medals" that hang on my neck and arms all day long—and a love for Christ that shapes my character every day! God really is the ultimate Coach who knows His players well and prepares them in advance for what is to come.

God is more concerned with your character than with your success. Will you trust Him with your dreams?

"For I know the plans I have for you," declares the Lord.
Jeremiah 29:11

Finishing Strong

Rafer Johnson
U.S. Olympic Gold Medalist in Decathlon

Only those who dare to fail greatly can ever achieve greatly.
ROBERT F. KENNEDY

The title of my autobiography, *The Best That I Can Be,* is not just a catchy slogan, but a personal mantra of how I've tried to live my life for more than 70 years. As an athlete, husband, father and Christian, I've always tried to be my very best—with God's help. But you know what? It isn't always easy to be your best. Life brings ups and downs, peaks and valleys, good times and bad.

During the course of my career in athletics, I experienced success not only in track and field, but also in basketball, baseball and football. At UCLA, I was privileged to learn and train under two of the greatest coaching legends of all time, Elvin C. "Ducky" Drake (in track and field) and John Wooden (in basketball). Coach Drake and Coach Wooden were the first to instill in me this desire to pursue excellence in all my endeavors.

In 1956, during my junior year at UCLA, I qualified for the 1956 Melbourne Olympics in long jump and decathlon. An injury to my knee, however, forced me to pull out of the long jump. I won the silver medal in the decathlon, but I was disappointed with second place. Four years later in Rome, I competed in the decathlon once again and brought home the gold. As tradition dictates, I was crowned the "world's greatest athlete" for this accomplishment.

After winning the gold in 1960 at the age of 25, I retired from track and field to pursue a second career in acting, broadcasting, and community and political activism.

Let me just say a frank word about "retiring" from athletics. As many of you other retired athletes know, the transition to that "second" career isn't easy! Your identity for 20 to 30 years has been encapsulated in the title "athlete." You train, eat, sleep and prepare full time to be the very best in your sport. And when God calls you to another vocation, the transition can be a difficult one. It was for me. I reached the peak of my athletic career when I was in my twenties! I then had to ask myself, *Okay, I have a lot of living left to do. How am I going to finish strong and be the best I can be in whatever God calls me to next?*

Don't be mistaken: I still need God's help to do my best. I can't do my best without Him. After years of grueling workouts and strict preparation, I was physically ready to do my best in 1960. But I still remember praying with Coach Drake before my event that God would give me peace and courage. On my knees, I asked the Lord to help me be the best that I could be. I knew that all of my talents and all of my skills weren't sufficient. I needed God to come alongside me. I never asked the Lord for victory. I just asked Him to help me be the best that I could be.

Whatever stage of life you're in, do your very best. Give back to your community. Make a daily commitment to faith. With God's help, I pray that you will finish your "race" with the assurance and hope that God runs with you.

Let us throw off everything that hinders and the sin that so easily entangles, and let us run with perseverance the race marked out for us.
HEBREWS 12:1

1 2

The Power of Influence

David Robinson
San Antonio Spurs MVP
Three-time U.S. Olympic Basketball Medalist

What we do now echoes in eternity.
GENERAL MAXIMUS, IN *GLADIATOR*

Although I never played on his team, Coach John Wooden was someone I always respected. I first had the opportunity to meet him in college when I won a basketball award. We sat and talked for a little while. To see a man with that kind of heart and love for Christ, who was so tough minded and had nurtured so many lives while compiling such an incredible record of winning, was awe-inspiring. I admired his strong faith. He was just an incredible person. I always looked up to him.

Even before I became a Christian, I believed that you could be a winner in the right way. But most people believe that you have to be a jerk to win. By watching Coach Wooden, I saw that you could be a fierce competitor on the court while always valuing people. He translated an edge to the court better than any other Christian I've seen.

People always called me "soft" because I didn't hang out in nightclubs, do drugs, abuse alcohol and chase women. But on the court I was still a top contender. And I knew I could compete right because of Coach Wooden's example.

On the day I was saved in 1991, I told God, "Whatever I have is Yours. Wherever You want me to go, I'll go. Whatever You want me to do, I'll do." I realized that I had never really expressed gratitude to God for all that He had given me.

I have to keep my heart and mind open to His Holy Spirit. He wants us to understand what we have is His. God doesn't want us to throw money away but to invest it wisely in others.

Inspired by Matthew 5:14 and the image of being a light to the world, my wife and I sat down to brainstorm what we could do to impact our San Antonio community for a long time to come. We wanted to leave a legacy that would continue to build and strengthen people long after we are gone. I'm a teacher at heart. Together we decided, "Let's start a school and teach young people who don't have a chance for a good education everything we can while giving them a foundation in Scripture." Utilizing my God-given engineering skills, we built the Carver Academy, a state-of-the-art, inner-city school built around a basketball court.

We knew it was important to go beyond the ABCs of basic education. We also wanted to emphasize the importance of discipline and core values. Since Carver Academy opened its doors in September 2001, we've taken in lots of kids without any spiritual background and started them off with a strong daily chapel. Every Friday we do a Hallelujah Hop. The staff makes it fun for the kids and shows the students the relevance of God in their daily lives.

Our faith-based curriculum is a great complement to what a parent should be doing at home. I've always believed that parents are called to be the greatest role models in their children's lives.

Through my years in the NBA, I learned that some people are so successful at what they do, but they fail where it counts most—at home. Our vision was to provide an education that not only prepares children to work but also prepares them for success in family relationships and in the community.

Another great joy for me is mentoring younger professional athletes and getting them to understand the power of their influence. I'm starting a financial investment business to teach players how to give. That's where my heart is now: to see the impact they can have on the community with their potential. I'm training others to give intelligently.

There's no greater feeling than standing on the podium. Yet even though it's fantastic for the moment, winning a gold medal or championship is so temporary. It's fleeting glory. Giving and influence are solid. It lasts a lifetime. You become linked to others. It's something that lasts forever!

What are you doing to express gratitude to God? Are you a light, first in your family and then in your community? If not, feed the hungry, walk for cancer, smile at a homeless person and give them a clean blanket, or volunteer at a school. Use your gifts and your influence to be a bright light for God's glory.

In the same way, let your light shine before men, that they may see your good deeds and praise your Father in heaven.
MATTHEW 5:16

1 3

Greater Gold

Brandon Slay

U.S. Olympic Gold Medalist in Wrestling

God lets you excel so you can make Him known . . .
and He will make you good at something.

MAX LUCADO

I will never forget the moment. I was in Sydney for the 2000 Olympics, living out the most emotionally demanding night of my life. As everyone will tell you, I am an extremely intense competitor, and I had just finished the final for 76 kg freestyle wrestling. I wanted so badly to win the gold.

Earlier, I stepped onto the mat, absolutely determined to give my all in my last match. I desired to honor my country and pay everyone back for all they had done for me. I anticipated giving glory to God whose love had cleaned me up the year before and brought me to this wonderful achievement.

Yet much to my frustration, nothing turned out as I expected. My opponent was very difficult, and the referee's calls were clearly "unhelpful"—much to the visible anger of the U.S. wrestling team's officials in the audience. To add to the incredible tension already in the air, when it was over, it didn't seem over! So many people there watching disagreed with the scoring. But the result stood, and my dream was over: I got silver.

After each medal ceremony, our wrestling team and supporters got together to celebrate. But how could I celebrate the ending of my Olympic dream? To make matters worse, my teammate, who also competed that night, had won silver as well. There was no new gold tonight. America expects its Olympians to be winners. How could I face the crowd that had worked so hard for me, and then, when it counted, I had let them down?

But what about God? I had intended to give Him glory if I won. How could I do less now? I still needed to trust Him, even when it hurt.

So I dried my bitter tears, and with the silver symbol of my shame still around my neck, I went to the team celebration. They asked me to say something, but words wouldn't come. As I stood there in the silence, I just kept looking at that audience of over 100 people, many of whom had made real sacrifices to travel halfway around the world to come and support me. I looked into their eyes; I saw more than one set of tears. They weren't angry with me. They were hurting with me. Despite tonight's devastating results, they still supported me.

Suddenly, I found welling up in me a genuine gratitude. I just started thanking everyone I could think of. Words began tumbling out—how I would not have had the privilege of being an Olympian and winning a silver medal if it hadn't been for the help of an army of people who believed in me, who believed that I was worthy of the investment of their time, money and love. And in that moment, I finally realized that the greatest thing about my competitive sports career was not my shelf of trophies or even that silver medal around my neck, but the wonderful relationships with all these people that I'd had the privilege to build over the years. I thanked God for bringing such a fine group of people into my life, and for giving me the opportunity to understand that there is something greater than even the gold: the love Jesus has for us that we can share with one another.

At the media interview the next day, I gave my first of what would turn out to be many greater-than-gold messages. One reporter dismissed my comments with a snide, "What else can you say, since you don't have a gold medal." I didn't care what he thought. In the midst of my pain, I knew I had found real truth.

Forty-five days later, I was on the *Today Show* for the first and only award ceremony outside of the Olympic Games. My opponent in Sydney had tested positive for steroids and was stripped of his medal. Having competed hard but clean, I really had won the gold.

After the ceremony, some reporters asked me what my message was now. I said, "It's still the same. Gold medals are great, but a relationship with Jesus Christ is even greater."

Do you value the people around you? Are you stopping to make friends even as you keep striving for your goals? Does Jesus have a place in your life?

Everyone who competes in the games goes into strict training.
They do it to get a crown that will not last,
but we do it to get a crown that will last forever.
1 CORINTHIANS 9:25

Coming Home

Josh Davis
Three-time U.S. Olympic Gold Medalist in Swimming

What do we live for, if not to make life less difficult for each other?
GEORGE ELIOT

Looking back at my preparation for my second trip to the Games, it's amazing to me how God orchestrated and blessed the events that were about to unfold. I was swimming better than ever, and thankfully made the team to go to Sydney. While I was at the training camp in L.A., my wife was at home, nine months pregnant and due any day. I received special permission to fly home from training to witness the birth of my son Luke. After seeing our third beautiful child born in under three years, I promptly flew to Australia to join the team. God gave Shantel strength to care for the babies, and He gave me strength to race as the oldest man on the U.S. swim team.

Because swimming is one of the most popular sports in the Summer Olympics, we were treated like superstars for the whole month. My team elected me captain, and I swam lifetime bests, breaking American records. It was probably one of the most fun and exciting weeks of my life. But despite the beautiful venue, exotic scenery and fanfare, I didn't think about staying in Australia to enjoy the second half of the Games very long.

I knew that back home in Texas, Shantel was overwhelmed and exhausted taking care of our children, Caleb (age two), Abby (age one) and Luke (just one month old). So within hours of cheering on the team for the last session of swimming, I left the Village and flew home to be with Shantel and our children.

Needless to say, Shantel was more than elated to see me. After I kissed her, she promptly handed me our newborn baby, who was wearing a loaded diaper. I spent the next eight days trying to watch every bit of the second week of the Games that I could, often holding two babies on my lap simultaneously. I kept busy with feeding, cleaning, wiping and changing, all with the TV on in the background. Sharing in Shantel's sleep deprivation didn't seem quite as bad, thanks to 24-hour coverage of the Games.

At home, feeling mortal and tired as I watched my fellow Olympians perform on my little TV, I couldn't believe I had actually been there just days earlier, winning two silver medals. Gone were the free massages, free food, great naps, and the constant laughing and encouragement of teammates. Despite the extreme contrast, I had no doubt that I was right where I was supposed to be.

I was so grateful that my wife had sacrificed so much to enable me to do what I was called to do. She had given her all for me so that I could give my all for my country. Quickly returning to her side to help was nothing compared to her having three babies in less than three years. Knowing that helped me find just as much joy changing diapers as I did leading the cheers for our team (well, almost—some of those diapers were pretty messy!). I'm glad I served my team in Sydney, but it was also important to serve my family back home.

When faced with selfish desires that conflict with commitments to family, friends and your relationship with God, what choices are you making? Are you willing to make sacrifices in order to experience the greater blessing?

Do everything in love.
1 CORINTHIANS 16:14

A Champion for Others

Josh Davis

Three-time U.S. Olympic Gold Medalist in Swimming

Do all the good you can, by all the means you can,
in all the ways you can, in all the places you can, at all the times you
can, to all the people you can as long as you can.

JOHN WESLEY

On June 13, 1936, Don Lash of Indiana did the unthinkable: He broke a world record that everyone thought was unbeatable, the two-mile time set five years before by Paavo Nurmi of Finland. On July 13, Don set a new American record in the 10,000 meters, finishing 140 yards ahead of the next competitor and qualifying for the 1936 Olympics.

But on July 12, Don Lash did the inconceivable. In the new Randall's Island, New York, stadium, he was competing in the final Olympic trials for the 5,000 meters, the Olympic event closest to his world record in the two-mile.

Don set a solid pace, and by the two-third's mark, he had built up a 40-yard lead. But it was a hot day, and some of the runners were struggling. In fact, 4 of the 12 wouldn't be able to finish the race. Don broke the first rule of competition: He looked back to see how the others were doing. Then he broke the second rule of competition: He became concerned about one of them, his good friend and fierce competitor, Tom Deckard. As teammates at Indiana, they had pushed each other hard in practice, with Tommy often winning. When Don had won his berth on the U.S. team in the 10,000 meters, Tommy had finished fourth, just missing qualifying for the Games in Berlin. This July 12 race was his last chance. And Tommy wasn't doing well. He was at the back of the pack of those still in contention.

Then Don, the "Iron Man from Indiana," broke the mold. In an Olympic trial, in his best event, his best chance at an Olympic medal, his best shot at fulfilling his dream and satisfying the expectations of a demanding nation . . . Don let four runners pass him as he dropped back to his younger teammate. He turned to his good friend and fierce competitor and said, "Come on, Tommy, you can do it. Just stay with me."

With three laps to go, Tommy stayed with Don, and Don stayed with Tommy. And one by one, the two of them together passed the other competitors. On the back stretch of the last lap, they took the lead, but at the head of the home stretch, Louis Zamperini challenged the pair, passing them both.

As the finish line approached and Tommy was assured of at least third place, qualifying him for the U.S. team, Don at last turned on his kick. He sprinted with Zamperini for 220 yards in a dead heat, tying for first by sticking out his barrel chest at the tape. As Arthur Daley of the *New York Times* put it, Don had won not one place but two.

Any competitor will tell you that in the heat of competition, you don't have time to contemplate whether you should do this or that. Don Lash didn't have time to think through what he was doing that day at Randall's Island. He had spent years training his heart to love others while training his body to lead all his competitors. And in a race where everything was on the line, Don Lash was true to his training in both.

Let us not love with words or tongue but with actions and in truth.
1 JOHN 3:18

Conclusion

We all recognize moments of greatness when we see them. It takes our breath away to witness people achieving a level of excellence that few others have ever accomplished.

Of course, the only thing better than seeing someone else's moment of greatness is garnering that greatness for ourselves. After all, it's only human nature to want to feel better about who we are by comparing ourselves to others we think are not as good at something as we are. Who doesn't want to be the best at something? Who hasn't dreamed about having the glorious spotlight shining on them, to be described as "super mom," "ultimate salesperson," "world-class athlete," "most beautiful" or "hall of famer"?

To aspire to greatness is one thing, but to become its slave is quite another. Some folks become absolutely fixated on winning human glory. They spend countless hours dreaming of exceeding everybody else so that they can bask in the awe and adulation of those around them. They long for their name to be the one floating around corporate offices, athletic facilities, professional conventions, church functions or moms' groups as the best—the very best. Driven to prove their superiority, they are willing to cut every corner, stampede over everyone else and even break the law to get there.

We all know the sad stories of people who have gone to extremes to secure their own personal glory, wealth, reputation, and so on. Athletes have tainted their careers by using steroids. CEOs have destroyed their companies by "fudging" the numbers for short-term financial gain. Parents have even driven their children in academics and extracurricular activities to the point of burnout, just so that the parents could be envied by their friends and neighbors.

As Christians, however, we are called to be different. We are never to seek to glorify ourselves. We are to seek to experience God's glory firsthand and then share it with others.

But how can human beings today witness the greatness of God? By holding on to the promise God gave to Moses: "I will cause all my goodness to pass in front of you, and I will proclaim my name, the LORD, in your presence" (Exodus 33:19). When we become His children through Jesus, God reveals His gracious goodness personally to each one of us. As our Savior begins to straighten out the issues in our lives, we begin to see firsthand His greatness, which cheers our hearts and puts light in our eyes.

Now as members of His family, we are privileged to freely bask in the blessings of His presence. We don't need to rush to desperately grab at them. As we stay close to God, we find the light of His glory penetrating even the darkest parts of our selfish human hearts, conforming us more and more to the image of our heavenly Father. The more time we spend with Him, the more we find ourselves becoming like Him. We grow to love Him more, and soon we are welcoming others into His presence. By continuing to abide in His presence in all circumstances, we radiate His glory to others, just like Moses did to the Children of Israel.

This truth became clear to me after I watched my first child being born. The nurses cleaned him up and placed him in a crib under a heat lamp—no clothes, no blankets, no socks . . . nothing but his bare skin. Like other first-time dads, I expressed concern to the nurse that he might get cold and potentially sick. However, the nurse just patted my arm and reassured me that he would be fine as long as he stayed under the lamp.

In the same way, as children of God, we don't need to "clothe" ourselves in titles, awards and positions to experience health and the "warmth" of wholeness—we just have to stay in the light of His glorious presence.

Yet so often we walk away from God's presence. And when we do, we inevitably begin to feel the chill of the world's cutthroat rivalries and foolishly grasp for what we think will bring us warmth—our *own* glory.

The athletes in this book have fought hard to be different. As Christians, they have made it their goal to pursue excellence without becoming addicted to worldly fame and fortune. Their moving stories testify that a gold medal doesn't warm the deepest places of the human heart. After all, an Olympic medal still feels cold to the touch, even when it is hanging around your neck!

They have also learned that no matter how much you achieve, you always need the inner presence of God to be whole. That's why these athletes have trained their hearts to look to God and bask in the glory of His loving goodness, instead of in their own achievements. As a result, they know now how to enjoy the journey with God, whether in plenty or want. They are fulfilling their calling, with contentment, using their successes and failures in sports to serve others in life, just like Jesus did.

What, then, is the secret to the success of the world-class champions in this book? In a nutshell, they have learned that *the glory is not about them!* They glory not in the strength of their own willpower but in the wonder of God's will to accomplish in and through them the good works He purposed for them before the foundation of the world.

We truly honor God's glory when we acknowledge our utter dependence on Him to finish the work He created us to do. Jesus glorified God by abiding in His presence and depending on His promises—not by offering up to Him worldly prizes. By His grace, let's commit ourselves to do likewise.

Closing Ceremonies

Josh Davis

As the 1996 Olympic Games approached their end, I became very nostalgic. The competitions were completed, all the awards had been given out and the flame burning in the stadium was soon to be extinguished. I thought of all the friends and family who had helped me get here, who had cheered me on, and I reflected on how thankful I was for them. I wondered in amazement how I had just raced in front of all those people. I pondered, *I hope God is pleased.*

And before I knew it, the closing ceremonies were at hand. The final big event was basically one giant concert with music and dancing and celebrating. The Olympians finally relax, taking a break from all the hard work they've done the last four years. But as the music ends and the flame is finally extinguished, every athlete's thoughts turn to what comes next, wondering, *What from this incredibly wonderful but very short time will last longer than the Games themselves?*

In the silence of my room that night, I thought about the glory of achievement that Olympians experience. And I had to admit, no matter how wonderful my medals were, the heroes of these Games would be replaced by the champions of the next. Athletic fame does not last forever—often not even four years! That's when I realized that it's not so much what you have done that will last long after the flame has been put out, but who you've become as a person, how you've grown in character through all the struggles—in short, how much you have fulfilled your potential as a human being.

Which is why the athletes who have shared their stories here have sought to help you focus on your personal growth.

We know that the only thing that matters in life is fulfilling the unique purpose God created for you and you alone. We want you to take an honest look at where you are in life, seek His guidance and then put into action the game plan of these Olympians: *Go for the goal, get some guts, and give God the glory.*

Whether in sports or in life, we all need an identity and a destination on the road to greatness. Setting *goals* (godly goals, because we are God's children) will help us experience the very best He has for us.

But please remember, the journey is going to be difficult. To reach your full potential is going to be the hardest thing you'll ever do. The road will be filled with obstacles and objectors to your dream, so you will need to get some *guts*. Always remember, you can find the courage and motivation you need from leaning on your travel companion, God Himself, the Holy Spirit.

And finally, know that when you use your talents to "make a big deal out of God," you will make an impact that lasts longer than just tonight's ESPN highlight tape. You see, knowing who you are in Christ gives you the freedom to risk everything, because even the immense pain of defeat doesn't have the last word. God will make something beautiful out of the broken, shattered, jagged edges of our dreams. And living that truth is the greatest way we can give God *glory*.

But to follow any of this advice, you have to first *get on the team*! Maybe you are reading this book and don't have a relationship with Jesus Christ like these athletes whose stories you've read. Well, if you'd like to be on their team, the best team, the real Dream Team, then it all starts with a simple prayer.

Praying to God is not so much the words you use as it is the attitude of your heart. And if this prayer reflects your heart's desire, say it out loud and trust God's faithfulness to hear you.

Heavenly Father,
I trust You. Thank You for loving me despite the many times
I have disappointed You. I confess that I have rebelled against
Your authority and made up my own rules to suit myself.

As a result, I have offended You, hurt other people and let myself down. Remembering my sins fills me with regret, but I am powerless to change my situation. I am now not fit to be a part of Your eternal family. But in Your great love for me, You sent Your Son, Jesus Christ, to take my punishment in my place so that I can share His right-standing with You instead.

For Jesus' sake, please forgive me all that is past. For His sake, please fill me full of Your Holy Spirit now and in the future. From this day forward, give me the power to lead a new life as a member of Your family, following You in Your service and loving You and all You have made. I ask this because I love You and want Jesus Christ to be my personal Savior and Lord now and forever. Thank You for hearing me and sending Him into my life, for it is through Him that I have prayed. Amen.

Congratulations! If you prayed this prayer with an honest heart, you are now a new creation. You're on a new team, and a new set of motivations is beginning to operate within you! As exciting as the Games are, they pale in comparison to the knowledge of eternal security. To know why you're here on Earth, and to know where you are going when you die, is maybe the most exciting truth a human can receive!

So in the midst of the ups and downs of life—and the fleeting moments of fame—cling to the beautiful knowledge that the power of God's love lasts longer than life itself. In fact, God is now working day by day to sustain in your heart a love for Him that eclipses your attachment to the world and its passing pleasures. And one day in the life to come, you will love God as perfectly as He loves you. That's God's greatest glory—that he is re-creating you and me to shine more and more perfectly with His love—forever!

The Coca-Cola motto for the Athens Olympics was "Live Olympic"—the company wanted to encourage people to live life big, bold and with purpose. Now that you have become a Christian, your job is to "Live Jesus!" which means following God's call wherever that may lead. It may mean pursuing excellence to the point of winning at the next Olympics. Of course, it may mean the exact opposite—the absence of worldly accolades—just rejoicing at what the Father is able to accomplish through you, just like Jesus did.

Therefore, no matter how many—or how few—medals God may bring your way, always remember to cling to the cross of Christ. On its hard wood, God proved His love for you. And only living in, through and for that love will give meaning to everything you do.

May God give you the guts to have as your goal to seek to know His glory and share it with others!

Live Jesus!

Brandon Slay

Vonetta Flowers

Matt Hemingway

Peter Westbrook

ATHLETE PROFILES

Brooke Abel

Birthday: February 15, 1988
Birthplace: Northridge, CA
Height: 5' 5"
Sport: Synchronized Swimming
Olympics: Has been selected for Team USA in Beijing 2008

Career

It didn't take Brooke Abel long to establish herself on the national scene. At the young age of 13, she captured four medals at U.S. Age Groups. In her first Junior National Championship appearance in 2002, she finished in the top two for Trio and ninth in the Team event. That same year Brooke earned first place in Team and second place in Solo and Duet at U.S. Age Groups. Brooke competed in her first U.S National in 2003 while continuing to compete in the Junior National Championships. In 2006, Brooke performed a triple gold-medal finish by earning first in Team, Solo and Duet. Recently Brooke was named to the 2007 U.S. Pan American and 2008 U.S. Olympic teams.

Personal

Julie and Eric Abel, Brooke's parents, quickly recognized that Brooke had a gift in synchronized swimming. They structured her schedule so that she could travel three hours round-trip to practice each day and also get in her studies at home. Their desire through home-schooling was to set their daughter up for success in all areas of her life. Their community and church in Fallbrook, California, have been very supportive.

Spiritual

"Every morning when I jump in the pool to do my laps, I have a prayer time with God. That's my time to reflect on the day and talk to God. I'm very blessed to have my teammate, Becky Kim, to look up to and share a kindred spirit. We often go to church together. Although I'm the youngest on the team, I lead prayer before our competitions."

Giving Back

Brooke helps with synchronized-swimming camps for young people.

Jennifer Barringer

Birthday: August 23, 1986
Birthplace: Webster City, IA
Height: 5' 5"
Sport: Track
Event: Steeplechase
College: University of Colorado, Boulder, CO
Olympics: 2008 Olympic contender

Career
Jennifer Barringer is an athlete of true determination. Her achievements include her most recent win of the 3,000-meter steeplechase championship at the NCAA Outdoor Track & Field Championships in June 2006. This was also her first All-American honor as a Buffalo, and she set the new school record of 9:53.04. Barringer won the NCAA Midwest Regional Crown and placed second at the Big 12 Championships in May. She placed third and tenth in the last two Foot Locker cross-country nationals and collected six state titles in high school and the Florida 6A cross-country title.

Personal
Jennifer is a freshman in college, but she has the determination of someone far older. She is a native of Oviedo, Florida, and she enjoys playing piano, traveling to run and studying in school to pursue a political career. She overcame a terminal respiratory illness as a child and has turned into one of the nation's most promising young athletes.

Spiritual
It would be easy for anyone with talents like Barringer to find strength in herself, but she has learned to depend on God. She really felt a difference in her life when she began to not only ask for His blessing, but also to praise Him for the talents He's given her. "I thanked God for creating me to run," she said before she won the NCAA Outdoor Championships. "When I humbled myself to praise Him, I found confidence to succeed without earthly pride."

Giving Back
Jennifer had to have surgery on her jaw in 2006. During this time, she decided to learn sign language to better communicate with others—and then used her new skills to minister to the deaf at her church in Oviedo.

Amanda Borden

Birthday: May 10, 1977
Birthplace: Cincinnati, OH
Height: 5' 4"
Sport: U.S. Gymnastics
College: Arizona State University
Olympics: 1996 U.S. Women's gymnastics team captain, gold medalist

Favorite Moment at the Games
"Sharing the top podium, as a team, during the medal ceremony was extra special as we reflected on the journey of getting to this moment."

Career
Amanda experimented with other sports, including ballet, until she started gymnastics in 1984. She was a six-time U.S. Women's National team member, Pan American double gold medalist and 1995 USAG Sportswoman of the Year. In 2006, Amanda was inducted into the U.S.A. Gymnastics Hall of Fame. She is a gymnastics commentator for CBS Sports, Fox Sports, Turner Broadcasting and ESPN.

Personal
Amanda is recognized for her high-voltage smile. In high school, she was a straight-A student and was elected Homecoming queen. "After reaching the pinnacle of my gymnastics career at just 19, I wondered, *What is left?* But marrying my husband, Brad, in 2006 and having a baby is even so much better." Amanda earned a summa cum laude B.S. in early childhood education from Arizona State University.

Spiritual
"Looking back, I really appreciate the spiritual foundation that my parents gave me. I grew up in a Christian home and went to church my whole life. When you have God behind you, that's a lot!" Her coach, Mary Lee Tracy, also had a profound influence on Amanda spiritually.

Favorite Scripture Verse
Philippians 4:13: "I can do everything through him who gives me strength."

Giving Back
"My goal is to touch the lives of children all across Arizona to help them reach their goals, whatever they may be." In 2004, she opened the

Gold Medal Gymnastics Academy in Tempe, Arizona, which trains over 650 gymnasts annually. "I also enjoy being involved in Special Olympics. I'm moved every time I watch these special kids overcome such tremendous obstacles." Check out www.goldmedalgym.com.

Annett Davis

Birthday: September 22, 1973
Birthplace: Long Beach, CA
Height: 5' 11"
Sport: Beach Volleyball
College: UCLA
Olympics: 2000 Olympic beach volleyball

Favorite Moment at the Games
"Walking into the stadium at Bondi Beach for the first time and playing in front of 10,000 people. Hearing the fans cheer for the United States and knowing that it was me representing our country was an amazing feeling."

Career
At UCLA, Annett received All-League and All-American honors. In 1994, she was the PAC-10's Player of the Year. She helped lead the United States to the four-person title at the 1997 FIVB Beach Volleyball World Championships. Annett and her partner, Jenny Johnson Jordan, have the longest-standing partnership on the AVP tour and a deep friendship. In 1999, they won more than any other U.S. men's or women's pro beach duo, with over $200,000 in prize earnings. After finishing fifth in the 2000 Olympics, they did not tour during 2001 or 2005 due to the birth of their children. But 2002 was their most successful AVP season as they gained two first places, two second places and three third places. They are best known for ending Kerri Walsh and Misty May-Treanor's 89-match winning streak. In 2007, they won the Chicago Open.

Personal
Sports runs in the family. Annett's dad, Cleveland Buckner, played for the New York Nicks in 1961. Her husband, Byron, missed the

1996 Olympic swimming team by three-tenths of a second and held a world record in the 50-meter butterfly. "I home school my children, Mya and Victoria, because I believe that there is no better teacher than your own mother, and no one cares about their development, spiritual growth and education nearly as much as I do."

Favorite Tune
"I've Been Looking for You" by Kirk Franklin

Spiritual
"First of all I am a child of God, a daughter of the King."

Favorite Scripture Verse
Proverbs 31:30: "Charm is deceptive, and beauty is fleeting; but a woman who fears the LORD is to be praised."

Giving Back
Realizing the importance of fitness, Annett is piloting a new program called Fit Moms-Fit Kids.

Josh Davis

Birthday: September 1, 1972
Birthplace: San Antonio, TX
Height: 6' 2"
Sport: Swimming
College: University of Texas
Olympics: 1996 Olympic gold medal in 400-meter free relay, 800-meter free relay and 400-meter mixed relay; 2000 Olympic silver medal in 800-meter free relay and 400-meter free relay

Favorite Moment at the Games
"Winning my first gold medal."

Career
After a storied prep career at Churchill High School in San Antonio, Josh was selected captain of the first USA Junior Swim team in

1990. That same year, he entered the University of Texas and was a major point contributor as the Longhorns went on to claim their fourth consecutive NCAA Swimming Championship. During his 4-year career at the University of Texas, he earned All-American honors 23 times. Serving as team captain in his final event, Josh and his teammates broke the Amer-ican record in the 4x100-yard free relay. After narrowly missing out in his attempt to qualify for the 1992 Barcelona Olympic Games, Josh made history four years later. Competing in the 400-meter free relay, 800-meter free relay and 400-meter mixed relay, he was the only man in the world to win three gold medals in Atlanta. In his last Olympic Games in Sydney, Australia, he brought home two silver medals while breaking the American record in the 200-meter freestyle three different times.

Personal
Josh is married to Shantel Davis, and they have five children (Caleb, Abby, Luke, Annie and Liam). They met at the University of Texas where Shantel was a standout volleyball player. His parents are Joan and Mike Davis, and he has three younger siblings (Will, Sam and Tynan).

Favorite Tune
"Dive" by Stephen Curtis Chapman

Spiritual
"God and sports not only can go together, they need to go together. Only developing the spirit and the body together can bring out the best in each."

Favorite Scripture Verse:
Romans 8:35: "Who shall separate us from the love of Christ?"

Giving Back
Josh participates in Fellowship of Christian Athletes, Athletes in Action, San Antonio Sports Foundation, and Mutual of Omaha BREAKout! Swim Clinic.

Allyson Felix

Birthday: November 18, 1985
Birthplace: Los Angeles, CA
Height: 5' 6"
Sport: Track and Field
Events: 100, 200, 400 meters
College: University of Southern California
Olympics: 2004 U.S. Olympic silver medalist, 2008 contender

Career
The future of American track and field looks very bright with sprinter Allyson Felix emerging as one of the sport's most promising young stars. In 2007, Allyson became only the second female athlete in history to win three events at the IAAF World Championships, taking home gold in the 200-meter, 4x100 meter relay and 4x400 meter relay. She also became the first woman in 12 years to defend her 200-meter World title. The youngest member of Team USA in 2004, 18-year-old Allyson won a silver medal at the Athens Olympics. As a high school senior, she ran the fastest 200-meter in history for a high school female, in addition to winning her fifth California State High School Championship title. Upon graduation, Allyson decided to forego her collegiate eligibility and signed a lucrative endorsement contract with Adidas.

Personal
Allyson didn't start running competitively until the ninth grade, but was soon after nicknamed "Chicken Legs" by her teammates at Los Angeles Baptist High School. Allyson was featured in one of Adidas's "Impossible Is Nothing" commercials. She was coached by Bob Kersee (husband of track legend Jackie Joyner-Kersee) and is currently majoring in Elementary Education at USC. Allyson's father is an ordained Baptist minister.

Spiritual
"My speed is definitely a gift from Him, and I run for His glory. Whatever I do, He allows me to do it."

Favorite Scripture Verse
Philippians 1:21: "For to me, to live is Christ and to die is gain."

Jennie Finch

Birthday: September 3, 1980
Birthplace: La Mirada, CA
Height: 6' 1"
Sport: Softball
College: Arizona
Olympics: 2004 U.S. Olympic gold medalist in softball

Favorite Moment at the Games
"Winning the gold medal."

Career
After a stellar high school career in La Miranda, California, Jennie moved on to play for the University of Arizona. While there, she established herself as one of the all-time greats in college softball. While leading the Wildcats to four consecutive College World Series appearances (including one National Championship in 2001), she was recognized as an All-American three times. In 2001, she completed arguably the greatest pitching season in college softball history. In that remarkable year, she compiled a perfect 32-0 record (an NCAA record) and was named the MVP of the College World Series. She also holds the NCAA record for consecutive wins (60) and recently had her #27 retired at the University of Arizona. Jennie has continued her success since moving into the professional ranks. She was a key member of the U.S. softball team as they claimed the gold at the World Championships in 2002. She followed that up with a gold medal the next year at the Pan Am Games and pitched Team USA to Olympic gold in 2004.

Personal
Jennie is the daughter of Bev and Doug Finch. She has two brothers, Shane and Landon. Her husband, Casey Daigle, is a pitcher in the Arizona Diamondbacks organization and the couple resides in Tucson, Arizona. They have a son who is fittingly named Ace. She currently works for ESPN.

Spiritual
"My faith has affected my career greatly. Without it, I would not be who I am today. God gave me this talent to use and He helps me daily to continue to pursue His will."

Favorite Scripture Verse

Philippians 4:13: "I can do everything through him who gives me strength."

Giving Back

Jennie is a spokesperson for KinderVision (National Child Safety Education Program) and Kids FIRST in Sports.

Vonetta Flowers

Birthday: October 29, 1973
Birthplace: Birmingham, AL
Height: 5' 7"
Sport: Track/U.S. Olympic bobsled team
College: University of Alabama
Olympics: 2002 U.S. Olympic gold medalist in bobsled, 2006 U.S. bobsled team

Favorite Moment at the Games

Although winning the gold medal and being chosen to carry the Olympic flag in the 2002 Olympic Games' closing ceremonies were special moments, Vonetta cherishes this as her favorite: "Kleenex, one of my sponsors, surprised me at the 2006 Games by flying my boys over to the Olympics. They were supposed to be in Florida with their grandmother, but while I was being interviewed by Katie Couric on the *Today Show*, I was extremely excited to see my twin sons, Jaden and Jorden, walk around the corner with big smiles on their faces."

Career

After injuries prevented the seven-time All-American track star from reaching the Summer Olympics, her husband, Johnny, played a vital role in her transition to the Winter Olympics. With just two weeks of training as the brakeman, she broke the world start record in 2000, and went on to win four World Cup medals, finishing in the top ten in all seven World Cup races in the bobsled. After taking 2006 to 2008 off to focus on her family, she plans to compete in the 2010 Games.

Personal

One week after the 2002 Winter Olympics' closing ceremonies, she became pregnant with fraternal twins. Born 10 weeks premature, Jorden weighed less than three pounds at birth and was completely deaf; however, a miraculous surgery in 2006 changed his life. Read Vonetta's book, *Running on Ice*, for more of her inspirational story.

Favorite Tune

"Never Give Up!" by Yolanda Adams

Spiritual

"I didn't grow up in a churched background, but my husband, Johnny, was a preacher's kid. Through my Olympic experiences, I've discovered that God's Word remains unchanged. He continues to love me unconditionally, even when I'm unwilling to trust Him 100 percent in every situation."

Favorite Scripture Verse

Matthew 22:14: "For many are invited, but few are chosen."

Giving Back

Through Jorden's fight to hear, Vonetta has been involved in supporting March of Dimes, Salvation Army, Susan G. Komen and Clarke-Jacksonville (Oral Auditory Program). Check out her website: www.von ettaflowers.com.

Matt Hemmingway

Birthday: October 24, 1972
Birthplace: San Pedro, CA
Height: 6' 7"
Sport: U.S. High Jump
College: University of Arkansas
Olympics: First alternate on 1996 U.S. track and field team, 2004 U.S. silver medalist in high jump

Favorite Moment at the Games

"That morning before the finals, I sat outside on the deck and listened to Switchfoot during my worship time with God. I thought about Eric Liddell . . . this is what I was made to do. I wasn't expected to medal. I decided to lay it on the line and skipped jumping at 7' 6" to attempt 7' 8" instead. That was the turning point. I was in the gold medal spot until the last jump when I missed three times at 7' 8", taking the silver."

Career
Matt first attempted the high jump in third grade and cleared 6' 10" by his junior year of high school. He turned down full athletic scholarships to join the dominant University of Arkansas Track and Field team under Coach McDonnell. There Matt became a four-time All-American and member of seven National Championship titles. Tired of the sport, he skipped competing in 1998 and 1999 to work as a guide at Noah's Ark White Water Rafting. He started jumping again for fun in 2000, training part-time in addition to holding a full-time sales management job. Amazingly he set three personal records in addition to having the highest indoor jump in the world that year at 7' 9", earning him the 2000 U.S. Indoor title. Matt had a strong season in 2005, highlighted by his win at the U.S.A. Outdoor Champion-ships. In February 2007, after sitting out the entire 2006 season with a foot injury, Matt took fourth at the U.S. Indoor Championship.

Personal
Matt was short in seventh grade, but grew to 6' 6" before graduating from high school. His favorite training methods are playing basketball and running hills with his dog.

Favorite Tunes
"Beautiful Letdown," "Meant to Live" and "24"—all by Switchfoot; "40" by U2

Spiritual
Matt's parents demonstrated a strong Christian faith. During college, he struggled with his core beliefs. But reading books by Ravi Zacharias and Francis Schafer solidified his faith.

Favorite Scripture Verse
Philippians 3:10: "I want to know Christ and the power of his resurrection and the fellowship of sharing in his sufferings, becoming like him in his death."

Giving Back

Matt and his wife, Kate, adopted their daughter, Asha, from Ethiopia in 2007 and look forward to growing their family in the future. He enjoys helping at Noah's Ark White Water Rafting (www.noahsark.com) and at Compassion International.

Penny Heyns

Birthday: November 8, 1974
Birthplace: Springs (now the Gauteng province), South Africa
Height: 5' 7"
Sport: Swimming
College: Nebraska University
Olympics: 1992, 1996, 2000 Republic of South Africa swim teams, 1996 South Africa gold medalist in 100-meter and 200-meter breaststroke, 2000 South Africa bronze medalist in 100-meter breaststroke

Favorite Moment at the Games

"Winning my first gold. Though the second felt good too. The world record in the prelims of the 100-meter breaststroke [her first gold] was a highlight. Somehow world records always meant a lot since they ultimately reflect personal improvement and excellence."

Career

Penny started swimming at age 7. By 16, she had won the gold in the 100-meter and 200-meter breaststroke at Senior Nationals. At Nebraska University, she won NCAA titles in the 100-meter and 200-meter breaststroke. Penny became the first woman in the history of the Olympics to win both breaststrokes, winning gold medals in the 100-meter and 200-meter in Atlanta in 1996. She was South Africa's first post-apartheid Olympic gold medalist. At the 2000 Olympics, she won a bronze medal in the 100-meter breaststroke before retiring from competitive swimming in 2001. As the first swimmer ever to hold all three distance-records simultaneously, as well as five of the six breaststroke records, Penny is considered the greatest female breaststroke swimmer of all time. In 2007 she was inducted into the International Swimming Hall of Fame for holding more breaststroke world records (14) than any other swimmer in history, male or female.

Personal
She is a dynamic international speaker and cofounder of OmniShare.

Favorite Tunes
"Awesome God" and "Be Unto Your Name"

Spiritual
Penny rededicated her life to God in April 1997. "No gold medal or world record ever gave me the peace and sense of wholeness I have found in having an intimate relationship with the Creator of the universe."

Favorite Scripture Verse
Proverbs 3:5-6: "Trust in the LORD with all your heart and lean not on your own understanding; in all your ways acknowledge him, and he will make your paths straight."

Giving Back
"Live to be a blessing" is Penny's personal credo. "In order to be truly successful in life, one must give! One must 'SHARE'—an acronym for our company values, which are Spirit, Heart, Attitude, Respect and Equality." Check out her website: www.pennyheyns.com.

Rafer Johnson

Birthday: August 18, 1935
Birthplace: Hillsboro, TX
Height: 6′ 3″
Sport: Decathlete
College: UCLA
Olympics: 1956 U.S. silver medalist in decathlon, 1960 U.S. gold medalist in decathlon

Favorite Moment at the Games
"Winning the gold medal."

Career
Rafer competed in his first track meet in 1954 as a freshman at UCLA and broke the world record in only his fourth competition. In 1956, he won a silver medal in the decathlon in the Olympic Games. After car-

rying the American flag in the opening day ceremony at the 1960 Olympic Games in Rome, he went on to set an event record while winning the gold medal. Numerous honors followed the event, including being named the *Sports Illustrated* Athlete of the Year, and *Sport Magazine* Sportsman of the Year. Rafer was inducted into the National Track & Field Hall of Fame in 1974 and culminated his career by lighting the torch to open the 1984 Olympic Games in Los Angeles.

Personal
Rafer competed under legendary UCLA coaches Ducky Drake (track and field) and John Wooden (basketball) and continues to be inspired by his friend Robert F. Kennedy, whom he campaigned for in 1968. Rafer's brother Jimmy is a member of the Pro Football Hall of Fame, his son Josh was a PAC-10 champion in javelin, and his daughter Jenny Johnson Jordan competed in beach volleyball at the 2000 Olympic Games.

Spiritual
"On October 29, 1953, I realized that I could never be lined up with His will until I accepted His Son, Jesus Christ, by faith as my personal Savior. There wasn't much emotion as I did this, but later, when I realized that He was blessing my commitment in many ways, the tears really flowed. I don't know when I've ever felt happier."

Giving Back
A Peace Corps volunteer, Rafer also helped found the California Special Olympics.

Jenny Johnson Jordan

Birthday: June 8, 1973
Birthplace: Newport Beach, CA
Height: 5' 10"
Sport: Beach Volleyball
College: UCLA
Olympics: 2000 U.S. beach volleyball team

Favorite Moment at the Games
"Walking into the stadium for the opening ceremonies with the other U.S. athletes in front of over 100,000 people in the stands."

Career

Jenny Johnson Jordan ("Triple J") played volleyball at UCLA, where she earned All-League and All-American honors. After graduating, Jenny moved from the hard court to the sand as she teamed up with roommate and best friend Annett Davis on the AVP beach volleyball tour. They currently enjoy the longest-standing partnership in U.S. history, closing in on 100 tournaments together. At the 2000 Sydney Olympics, the tandem placed fifth. They enjoyed their most successful AVP season in 2002. Jenny has been ranked in the top five in season points during each of her Tour seasons. In August 2007, Johnson and Davis were crowned Chicago Open champions for the second consecutive season.

Personal

If success is in the genes, then Jenny was born to succeed. Her father is the legendary Rafer Johnson, her brother Josh was a PAC-10 champion in javelin, and her uncle is Pro Football Hall of Famer Jimmy Johnson. Jenny added to that gene pool when she married Kevin Jordan, a former wide receiver on the UCLA football team. Their daughter, Jaylen, was born in October 2001 and their son, Kory, in June 2005.

Spiritual

"As I experience my relationship with Christ, I constantly remind myself that my walk is truly a marathon and not a sprint. On a daily basis I experience peaks and valleys, but what remains the same is the knowledge and the faith that God is in control and He is with me every step of the way."

Jeremy Knowles

Birthday: August 30, 1981
Birthplace: Nassau, Bahamas
Height: 5' 10"
Sport: Swimming
College: Auburn University
Olympics: 2000, 2004 Bahamian swim team

Favorite Moment at the Games

"The opening ceremonies."

Career

Jeremy competed in his first swim meet at the age of five. A native of the Bahamas, he broke his first national record at the age of eight in the individual medley. Currently, he holds eight Bahamian national records. After graduating from St. Andrews School in 1999, he enrolled at Auburn University. While competing at Auburn, he garnered All-American honors a total of six times from 2002 to 2004. In that time, the Tigers also claimed two NCAA Team Championships (2003, 2004). In 2000, Jeremy competed for his native Bahamas in the Sydney Olym-pic Games and swam personal bests in three of his events. He also became the first Bahamian to compete in the World University Games in 2003. He brought home a bronze medal in the 200-meter butterfly at that competition. In 2003, he qualified for his second Olympic Games by meeting the qualifying mark in the 400-meter individual medley at the Pan Am Games held in Santo Domingo, Dominican Republic.

Personal

Jeremy's greatest claim to fame is likely his daring 30-mile ocean swim from Beacon's Bay, Exuma, to Yamacraw Beach, New Providence. The jaunt, which took more than 15 hours, established him as a national hero. He received the Ministry of Youth Sports and Culture Pace Setter Award in 1998. He married Heather Leigh on June 18, 2005.

Spiritual

"My father and Jesus have modeled for me how to live life to its fullest. Being a part of a swim team with other guys who don't have the same spiritual priorities put my faith to the test."

Giving Back

"I would like to give back to my country, the Bahamas, the first medal at a major international world-class swimming event."

Mark Knowles

Birthday : September 4, 1971
Birthplace: Nassau, Bahamas
Height: 6' 3"
Sport: Tennis
College: UCLA
Olympics: 1992, 1996, 2000, 2004 Bahamian Olympic tennis

Favorite Moment at the Games
"I always look forward to the opening ceremonies: the minute you walk into the stadium and they call your country. You're one of thousands of athletes being cheered by the fans. No matter how great you are, you're in awe of everyone else and the grandeur. I'm a boxing fan, so witnessing Muhammad Ali light the torch in Atlanta was probably my most memorable Olympic moment."

Career
At age 10, Mark trained at the famous Nick Bolleteri Tennis Academy. By 15, he became the U.S. Indoor 16s champion in singles, while also finishing as a runner-up in doubles. He earned All-American honors before joining the pro tour in 1991. In 1994 Mark partnered with Daniel Nestor, winning the first tournament they entered. By 2002 they ranked No. 1 in the world in tennis doubles after winning the Australian Open and making the finals of Wimbledon. The duo won the U.S. Open in 2004, adding the French Open Title in 2007. Mark has won 46 doubles titles. Wimbledon is the only Grand Slam that still eludes him. In 2006 he participated in the longest match in Wimbledon history—it lasted 6 hours and 9 minutes.

Personal
Mark started playing tennis at age four, coached by his parents who were tennis pros at a Nassau tourist resort. He met his wife, Dawn, on a plane. Their son, Graham, brings great joy to their lives.

Spiritual
"I was exposed to God at a young age though my family and continued to grow through FCA and church. As a tennis player, you can feel lonely because it's an individual sport. It's important to have a strong faith and foundation."

Favorite Scripture Verse
1 Corinthians 13:4: "Love is patient, love is kind. It does not envy, it does not boast, it is not proud."

Giving Back
Since 2001, Mark has hosted the Annual Mark Knowles Tennis Celebrity Invitational, as a fundraiser for Nassau charities. This event draws big names such as Andre Agassi, James Blake, Jim Courier and Tommy Haas. Check out his website: www.marknowles tennis.com.

Eric Liddell

Birthday: January 16, 1902
Birthplace: Tientsin, China
Height: 5' 9"
Sport: Track
College: Edinburgh University
Olympics: 1924 British Olympic gold medalist in 400-meter, bronze medalist in 200-meter

Winning the gold medal and breaking the world record in the 400-meter, an event that was not his best, was a consolation prize after Eric's decision that he could not run the 100-meter, his favorite, on Sunday, the Lord's day. He chose God over gold and in His goodness, God ultimately gave Eric both. He instantly became a national hero and raced and spoke throughout the United Kingdom for a full year.

Career
Although Eric had been a sickly and skinny child, when he was 12, his athletic talent emerged through cricket, rugby and track. Some of his high school track records still stand today, and many of his college records lasted for over 30 years. After three years on the mission field with limited training and racing, Eric ran a time trial the same week as the 1928 Amsterdam Olympics and his times would have won.

Personal
Eric's parents, James and Mary Liddell, were missionaries to China. Eric served on the mission field in China from 1925 to 1943. He married Florence in 1933, and they had three daughters.

Spiritual

Eric was very quiet and shy about his faith for many years until a college friend asked him to share his testimony at an outreach event. His vibrant faith was evident, as was his humble charisma and sense of humor. His ministry of teaching and speaking continued for 20 years. "He was truly committed to God and told people how God was totally committed to them."

Giving Back

Eric died from exhaustion at only age 42, serving the Chinese people and sharing the love of Christ. Because of his extraordinary life, orphanages, buildings at his alma maters and boys' clubs bear his name. Books and movies continue to be made about his amazing example of what Christ can do through us when we completely surrender to His will.

Barb Lindquist

Birthday: July 1, 1969
Birthplace: Wilmington, DE
Height: 5' 6"
Sport: Swimming and U.S. Triathlon
College: Stanford University
Olympics: 2004 Olympic triathlon

Favorite Moment at the Games

"During the race on the bike, working with my teammate Susan Williams, who went on to win the United States' first medal in triathlon history."

Career

Barb was a member of the 2004 U.S. Olympic team, placing ninth in Athens. She made history in 2002 and 2003 by capturing the Australian series title—a feat no non-Australian has ever done. Barb has been the U.S. Pro Champion, and every year since 1996, she has been a member of the World Championship team as a professional. Perhaps her most impressive accomplishment was holding her No. 1 world ranking longer than any other male or female in the sport.

Personal
Barb is married to coach Loren Lindquist, who has encouraged Barb and helped her achieve her great success. In 2007, Team Lindquist grew to four after Barb delivered twins. She enjoys taking her twins on a 90-minute bike ride each day.

Favorite Tune
"Smellin' Coffee" by Chris Rice

Spiritual
When Barb was 11, she asked the Lord into her heart. She says her biggest spiritual growth came after college and swimming, but before she became a triathlete. After struggling with self-confidence issues and feeling pressure to have perfect results in the classroom and out racing, she experienced a breakthrough. God finally "birthed a new desire to race again with a new freedom." She discovered His love was unconditional, regardless of how well she performed. This new freedom and confidence in Christ alone has allowed her to enjoy racing again and look at every race as an opportunity to praise Him with her talents.

Favorite Scripture Verse
Zechariah 4:6: " 'Not by might nor by power, but by my Spirit,' says the LORD Almighty."

Giving Back
Barb is involved with the Fellowship of Christian Athletes and is a sought-after public speaker. Check out her website at: www.barblindquist.com.

LaVonna Martin-Floreal

Birthday: November 18, 1966
Birthplace: Dayton, OH
Height: 5' 7"
Sport: Track and Field
Event: 100-meter hurdles
College: University of Tennessee
Olympics: 1988 and 1992 Olympics, 1992 U.S. Olympic 100-meter silver medalist

Favorite Moment at the Games

"At the time, winning the silver medal was my favorite moment. But I met Canadian Olympic long jumper, Edrick Floreal, at the Olympics. I wasn't looking for a husband at the time. But thanks to Madeline [Manning Mims], we were married five months after the Olympics. Looking back, meeting my husband in the Olympic Village was clearly my best memory. He competed in two Olympics for Canada in the long jump and triple jump."

Career

During her high school career (1981 to 1984), LaVonna set 17 meet records and three national high school records in indoor track. As a Lady Vol, she became a 14-time All-American. She won three individual and two relay NCAA events, set a Pan American Games record, and earned three national TAC 100 hurdles titles. She completed her career by placing second at the 1994 IAAF World Indoor Championships in the 60-meter hurdles.

Personal

Her husband is currently the Franklin P. Johnson Director of Track and Field at Stanford University. They have two children, both of whom are athletic as well.

Favorite Tune

"Let the Praise Begin" by Martha Munizzi

Spiritual

Although she grew up going to church and made a decision for Christ as a child, LaVonna primarily relied on her mother's faith until 1991, when she really grew in her personal relationship. Her church community was a refuge to her as she successfully fought illegal substance charges after she had unknowingly been given performance-enhancing drugs by her coach. "When God became the center of my life, I no longer relied on winning to define my identity and my value."

Favorite Scripture Verse

Philippians 4:6-7: "Do not be anxious about anything, but in everything, by prayer and petition, with thanksgiving, present your requests to God. And the peace of God, which transcends all understanding, will guard your hearts and your minds in Christ Jesus."

Giving Back
LaVonna enjoys teaching and making a difference as a middle school teacher at the Los Altos Christian School in Palo Alto, California.

Madeline Manning Mims

Birthday: January 11, 1948
Birthplace: Cleveland, OH
Height: 5' 9"
Sport: Track and Field, 440-meter, 800-meter
College: Tennessee State University
Olympics: 1968 U.S. Olympic track 800-meter gold medalist; 1972 U.S. Olympic silver medalist 1600-meter relay team; 1976 and 1980 U.S. Olympic track and field team

Favorite Moment at the Games
Winning the gold medal in the 800-meter in 1968 at the Olympic Games in Mexico City, becoming the first and only U.S. female to win the 800-meter in the history of the Olympic Games. Notably, Madeline was the first U.S. middle-distance runner to reach world-class caliber at a time when it was believed that African-Americans could only sprint. At age 32, she won all four of her events and was named Most Outstanding Female Athlete at the U.S. Olympic trials in 1980, but the U.S. boycott of the Moscow Games kept her from competing in her fourth Olympics.

Career
Madeline won her first national title in the 440-yard run at the girls' 1965 AAU championships. While still in high school, she was named to the U.S. team that competed in meets against the USSR, Poland and West Germany. She won 10 national indoor and outdoor titles and set numerous American records from 1967 to 1980. (As a senior in high school, she ran her first world indoor record in the women's 800-meter in Toronto, Canada.)

Personal
Madeline almost died of spinal meningitis when she was only three years old. Her daughter, Lana, has already won three Oklahoma State

Championship titles in both the long and high jumps, and she has also competed in the U.S. Junior Olympics. Read Madeline's inspiring autobiography, *The Hope of Glory*.

Favorite Tune
"My Tribute" by Andre Crouch

Spiritual
"My mom was a prayer warrior, and we were raised in the Baptist Church. I never knew what it was like to not have God in my life. When I was about six years old, I realized not everybody knew God and that I needed to personally make a decision. That's when I invited Christ into my life."

Favorite Scripture Verse
Philippians 1:6: "He who began a good work in you will carry it on to completion until the day of Christ Jesus."

Giving Back
Madeline is a talented gospel singer-songwriter, motivational speaker, author and ordained minister. She is completing a Masters of Divinity and ultimately a Doctorate of Ministry in Sports Chaplaincy. Having served as a chaplain at five Olympic Games, she is leaving an incredible legacy in her 40 years of ministering to world-class athletes.

John Naber

Birthday: January 20, 1956
Birthplace: Evanston, IL
Height: 6' 6"
Sport: Swimming
College: University of Southern California
Olympics: 1976 U.S. Olympic gold medalist in 100-meter and 200-meter backstroke, 800-meter freestyle relay, and 400-meter medley relay (all in world-record times); and silver medalist in 200-meter freestyle

Favorite Moment at the Games
"A favorite memory was traveling up the Village elevator surrounded by five other Olympians: a tall basketball player, a heavy weightlifter, a

tiny gymnast, a cauliflower-eared wrestler and a skinny long-distance runner. I realized how small the world really is."

Career

John was the first swimmer ever at the Games to win two individual medals on the same day. He served as an Olympic torchbearer four times, and was twice President of the U.S. Olympians. In 1984, he was inducted into the U.S. Olympic Hall of Fame. John captured 10 individual NCAA titles between 1974 and 1977, and received the James E. Sullivan award as America's top amateur athlete in 1977. John has covered over 35 different sports and 8 Olympic Games for television and radio. An author and motivational speaker, John teaches others how to set goals and achieve world-class results.

Personal

John lives with his wife, Carolyn, in Pasadena, California.

Spiritual

"In July 1976, knowing the Olympics were going to be a watershed moment for me, I wanted to be alone with my Lord. I went to Him in prayer somewhat fearful of the pressure of the Olympics. It marked a turning point in my life. God gave me real peace that His presence would be with me."

Favorite Scripture Verse

Romans 8:28: "We know that in all things God works for the good of those who love him, who have been called according to his purpose."

Giving Back

John's favorite charity is "Swim With Mike" (www.swimwithmike.org), a college scholarship fund for high school athletes who have been injured or disabled. Check out his website at: www.johnnaber.com.

Leah O'Brien-Amico

Birthday: September 9, 1974
Birthplace: Garden Grove, CA
Height: 5' 9"
Sport: U.S. Olympic Softball
Position: First Base (2004) and Outfield (1996-2000)
College: University of Arizona
Olympics: 1996, 2000, 2004 U.S. Olympic softball gold medalist

Favorite Moment at the Games
"My teammate Laura Berg got a hit that scored the winning run to help us win the gold medal (2000). Although very quiet about her faith, she told me it wasn't her that did it; it was God who helped her. My friendship had an impact."

Career
Leah pitched her way to her first national championship at 14 and went on to win three NCAA Championships (1993, 1994, 1997). As one of the top clutch hitters in the world, she still holds the Women's College World Series record for best batting average in one tournament, hitting .750 (9 for 12) in 1994. She was named the 1997 NCAA Arizona Woman of the Year, and she played on two World Championship teams (1998, 2002) and Pan American Games Championship teams (1999, 2003). Leah was a three-time First-Team NFCA All-American and three-time First-Team Academic All-American. In 2006, she was named to the NCAA Division I Softball 25th Anniversary Team.

Personal
During her team's trip to Guatemala in 1994, she discovered each day is a gift not to be taken for granted. She returned home very thankful for running water, clean shoes and food. Leah married her husband, Tommy, in 1999. She was the first mother on the U.S. Olympic Softball Team and has three sons: Jake (born in 2001), Drew (2005) and Luke (2007).

Favorite Tunes
"Holy Is the Lord" and "How Great Is Our God" by Chris Tomlin

Spiritual
Though Leah had attended church as a small child, softball had replaced her Sunday routine. Since she committed her life to Christ in college, Leah's priorities have been God first, family second and softball third.

Favorite Scripture Verse
Philippians 4:13: "I can do everything through him who gives me strength."

Giving Back
Athletes in Action is her favorite ministry. Leah is a host of the Trinity Broadcasting Network (TBN) show *More Than Conquerors* alongside Frank Pastore and A. C. Green. Check out her website: www.leah20.com.

John Register

Birthday: March 9, 1965
Birthplace: St. Louis, MO
Sport: Hurdles/Swimming
College: University of Arkansas
Olympics: 1996, 2000 Paralympics long jump silver medalist

Favorite Moment at the Games
"At the 1996 Paralympics, watching Gong win the gold medal in the 200-meter individual medley absolutely inspired me. Swimming without arms, he slammed the wall with his head each lap to meet regulations for touching the wall."

Career
John was a three-time All-American in the NCAA long jump and on the 4x400-meter relay teams. He qualified for the Olympic trials in hurdles in 1988 and 1992. During his service in the Army from 1988 to 1994, John participated in the Army's World Class Athlete Program, winning nine gold medals in Armed Service Competition.

Personal
On May 17, 1994, John injured himself doing routine hurdle training and severed an artery, ultimately leading to his leg being amputated

and ending his 1996 Olympic bid. His wife, Alice, was a tremendous support. During rehabilitation, he started swimming. Just 18 months later, John made the 1996 Paralympics team as a swimmer and set a goal of competing in track and field in 2000. At the 2000 Games in Sydney, Australia, he broke the American long jump record with a distance of 18.4 feet. John is a gifted inspirational and motivational speaker.

Spiritual
John's strong faith in Christ was an anchor during his recovery. "My continual life question is, *Am I on track?* I regularly take a look in the mirror of my heart to see if it's for His glory or for mine."

Favorite Scripture Verse
Philippians 4:13: "I can do everything through him who gives me strength."

Giving Back
John now works with the United States Olympic Committee (USOC) as the associate director for outreach and development, managing both the USOC Paralympic Military Program and the Paralympic Academy International. Check out his website at: www.johnregister.com or email him at: john@johnregister.com.

Ruth Riley

Birthday: August 28, 1979
Birthplace: Ransom, KS
Height: 6' 4"
Sport: Basketball
College: Notre Dame
Olympics: 2004 U.S. Olympic gold medalist in basketball

Favorite Moment at the Games
"Winning the gold medal on August 28 was the best present I ever dreamed for my twenty-fifth birthday."

Career
Ruth began her basketball career in the fourth grade and has been dominating the sport ever since. She started wearing her trademark

headband while playing in high school. Only six games into her freshman year at Notre Dame, she became a starter and the cornerstone of the program. After consecutive All-American campaigns (1999-2000, 2000-2001), she led the Fighting Irish to their first National Championship after sinking the decisive free throws with only 5.8 seconds remaining. Success followed Ruth to the professional ranks. After a brief stint with the Miami Sol (by which she was taken as the fifth overall pick in the WNBA draft), she joined the reeling Detroit Shock. In one of the great turnarounds of all time, she led them to the WNBA Championship in 2003, just one season after Detroit had claimed the worst record in the WNBA. In the championship series, she was honored as the MVP. The next year, she served our country proudly by leading the United States to a gold medal in basketball in the 2004 Olympic Games.

Personal
Basketball is definitely Ruth's passion, and she displays it in a number of different ways off the court. She wrote about it in her recently released children's book, *The Spirit of Basketball.*

Spiritual
"I have confidence in my game because I know God loves me regardless of my performance, and shapes me through my circumstances for His purpose."

Favorite Scripture Verse
Colossians 3:23: "Whatever you do, work at it with all your heart, as working for the Lord, not for men."

Giving Back
Ruth is involved in organizations that support youth development, literacy and athletics, including Athletes in Action, Orchards Children's Services, March of Dimes, Nothing But Nets (www.nothingbutnets.net) and WNBA Read to Achieve.

David Robinson

Birthday: August 6, 1965
Birthplace: Key West, FL
Height: 7' 1"
Sport: Basketball (San Antonio Spurs)
College: U.S. Naval Academy
Olympics: 1988 U.S. Olympic bronze medalist in basketball; 1992, 1996 U.S. Olympic gold medalist in basketball

Favorite Moment at the Games
"The thing that I remember the most from all of my experiences at the Games was going into the arena for the opening ceremony in Atlanta with all of the pomp and circumstance and 100,000 cheering fans. What a powerful thing sports is that it brings all of these people together."

Career
Although David was the NBA's top draft choice for 1987, the San Antonio Spurs waited until "The Admiral" completed his military pledge before signing him to the team. He was the only Naval Academy graduate in NBA history. Voted Rookie of the Year, he became a 10-time NBA All-Star. David is one of two players, along with Kareem Abdul-Jabbar, to win scoring ('94), rebounding ('91) and blocked-shots ('92) titles during his career. He even scored 71 points in one game.

Personal
From childhood David loved building things. He didn't play basketball until his senior year in high school, and he grew seven inches at the Naval Academy. He's a family man who enjoys spending time with his wife, Valerie, and sons, David, Jr., Corey and Justin. For fun David likes to indulge in video games.

Favorite Tunes
Worship Again album by Michael W. Smith; "Blessed Assurance," "Turn Your Eyes," "Take My Life" by Third Day; artist Donnie McClurkin

Spiritual

David's parents regularly took him to church growing up. However, he drifted away from his faith on the way to stardom. Despite money and success, he lacked purpose. In 1991 David and his future wife, Valerie, invited God into their lives and started an adventure of spiritual significance together. He served as Men's Ministry Leader and on staff at Oak Hills Church in San Antonio, Texas.

Favorite Scripture Verses

Matthew 6:33: "But seek first his kingdom and his righteousness, and all these things will be given to you as well."

Proverbs 3:5-6: "Trust in the LORD with all your heart and lean not on your own understanding; in all your ways acknowledge him, and he will make your paths straight."

1 Thessalonians 5:16-18: "Be joyful always; pray continually; give thanks in all circumstances, for this is God's will for you in Christ Jesus."

Giving Back

David believes that we've been put on this earth mostly to give back. In 1991 he started pledging college scholarships. David's $9 million gift to The Carver Academy, a faith-based school in San Antonio, was the largest donation ever made by a pro athlete. The NBA even renamed their monthly Community Assist award after David Robinson. Check out www.thecarveracademy.org.

Congressman Jim Ryun

Birthday: April 29, 1947
Birthplace: Wichita, KS
Height: 6′ 3″
Sport: Track and Field—the mile, 1,500-meter and 880-yard runs
College: University of Kansas
Olympics: 1964, 1968 U.S. silver medalist in the 1500-meter; 1972 U.S. track and field team

Favorite Moment at the Games

Jim's favorite moment took place during his first trip to the games in 1964, when he was a junior in high school. He won the silver medal in 1968, overcoming a pulled hamstring, mono and the 7,000-foot altitude of Mexico City. In his third Olympic Games in 1972, he was knocked unconscious when another runner tripped him.

Career

In 1964, Jim achieved national acclaim when he became the first high school student ever to break the four-minute mile with 3:59. He bettered his time to 3:55:30, a record that stood for 36 years. He received the *Sports Illustrated* Sportsman of the Year award for 1966, later earning many NCAA championship titles. Jim also held world records in the mile, 1,500-meter run and 880-yard run. First elected to Congress in 1996, he served five terms representing the Second Congressional District of Kansas. Jim was inducted into the Track & Field Hall of Fame in 2003. He was recently voted by ESPN as the Best High School Athlete Ever.

Personal

Jim and his wife, Anne, have four adult children—Heather, Drew, Ned and Catharine—and they live in Lawrence, Kansas. You'll be inspired by reading *The Courage to Run,* a practical devotional about winning the race of your life, written by Jim and his sons.

Favorite Tune

"Holy Is the Lord" by Chris Tomlin

Spiritual

On May 18, 1972, Jim and his wife, Anne, accepted Christ as their Lord and Savior. He still considers his salvation the best decision he ever made. Jim reflects, "Of all the races I have run, the most important race is the one I live each day for Christ."

Favorite Scripture Verse

John 3:3-8: "In reply Jesus declared, 'I tell you the truth, no one can see the kingdom of God unless he is born again.' 'How can a man be born when he is old?' Nicodemus asked. 'Surely he cannot enter a second time into his mother's womb to be born!' Jesus answered, 'I tell you the truth, no one can enter the kingdom of God unless he is born of water and the Spirit. Flesh gives birth to flesh, but the Spirit gives birth to spirit. You should not be surprised at my saying, "You must be born again." The wind blows wherever it pleases. You hear its sound, but you cannot tell where it comes from or where it is going. So it is with everyone born of the Spirit.'"

Giving Back

In 1975, Jim started the Jim Ryun Running Camps, a unique camp where instruction is geared toward developing the total runner—physically, mentally and spiritually. Check out Jim Ryun Ministries at: www.ryunrunning.com.

Matt Scoggin

Birthday: August 17, 1963
Birthplace: Great Falls, VA
Height: 5′ 10″
Sport: U.S. Diving
College: University of Texas
Olympics: 1992 U.S. Olympic diving team, 2000 U.S. Olympic assistant diving coach

Favorite Moment at the Games

"When everyone in the grandstand applauded me for getting back up again after my previous failed dive. I'll never forget that." Matt was selected as team captain at the 1992 Olympics and voted 1992 Athlete of the Year for diving by the U.S. Olympic Committee.

Career

A veteran Longhorn who competed for Texas from 1981 to 1985, Matt returned to Texas as an assistant coach in 1986. In his fourteenth season as Texas's head diving coach, Matt has clearly established the Longhorns as one of the nation's top men's and women's diving programs, winning 15 NCAA titles. He received the first-ever Benjamin Foundation Coaches Performance Award by USA Diving. In 2001 and 2002, he was voted the Men's NCAA Diving Coach of the Year. In 1997, 1998 and 1999, he was selected as both the NCAA Division I National Women's Diving Coach of the Year and the Big 12 Conference Women's Diving Coach of the Year, as well as adding league honors again in 2003. Fourteen divers under Scoggin's tutelage have captured an NCAA individual championship, including Olympic gold medalist Laura Wilkinson, Verya Ilyina (Russia) and Nicole Pohorenec. Matt's intense dedication to the sport and a keen technical eye have contributed to his success as a coach.

Spiritual

Matt's wife, Becca, has been a tremendous encouragement to him in life and in his faith journey. Although he was raised Catholic, he started attending church because of her and grew to a personal faith in 1993. His parents started going to church again after he qualified for the Olympics.

Favorite Scripture Verse

Psalm 136:26: "Give thanks to the God of heaven. His love endures forever."

Brandon Slay

Birthday: October 14, 1975
Birthplace: Amarillo, TX
Weight: 167.5 pounds
Sport: U.S. Freestyle Wrestling
College: University of Pennsylvania
Olympics: 2000 U.S. Olympic gold medalist in 76 kg. wrestling

Favorite Moment at the Games

"It was amazing to walk into the Olympic Stadium during the opening ceremonies with 110,000 people in the stands and 10,000 athletes making the walk around the track. I'll never forget the thrill of stepping onto the mat to represent our nation, the state of Texas, and my community of Amarillo. I received my gold medal 45 days after the Games on the *Today Show* in Rockefeller Center."

Career

When Brandon started wrestling at age six, he lost every match except one. As a high school freshman, he advanced to the Texas State Championship finals, followed by three State Championship titles. In college, his wrestling team went from ninetieth in the nation to ninth. Brandon placed second at the NCAA Championships twice and led UPenn to four Ivy championships. He was the Ivy Rookie of the Year in 1994 and the Ivy League Wrestler of the Year in 1997 and 1998. After he graduated from the prestigious Wharton School of Business, he put his business career on hold to move to the Olympic training center for a Freestyle Residency Program. He was the first native Texan ever to make the U.S. Olympic wrestling team and was the 2000 U.S. National Champion.

Personal
Brandon resides in Dallas, Texas, where he works in real estate.

Spiritual
Brandon closed 1999 by giving his life completely to Jesus Christ. His motto is, "Do your best and let God take care of the rest!"

Favorite Scripture Verse
Psalm 136:26: "Give thanks to the God of heaven. His love endures forever."

Giving Back
After the Games, Brandon started Greater Gold, which prepares youth to reach their full academic and athletic potential while planting positive seeds of biblical truth. He spends at least one night a week working with the Dallas Dynamite Wrestling Club. Check out his website: www.greatergold.com.

Ugur Taner

Birthday: June 20, 1975
Birthplace: Istanbul, Turkey
Height: 6' 2"
Sport: Swimming
College: University of California at Berkeley
Olympics: 1992 Olympics

Favorite Moment at the Games
Meeting athletes in the Olympic Village.

Career
Ugur started swimming competitively at the age of nine after his friend's mom (who happened to be a swim coach) asked him to join the team. The next year, he started swimming year round and the rest is history. While attending Newport High School in Washington, he won the gold medal at the 1990 U.S. Olympic Festival. The summer after his prep

career ended, Ugur swam for his native Turkey in the 1992 Olympic Games. While attending the University of California at Berkeley, he dominated the 200-yard fly, winning three consecutive NCAA titles (1994-1996). He became a member of the U.S. swim team in 1993 and won a gold medal in the World Championships in 1994 (4x100-meter free). In all, he collected six U.S. Championships including two in the 200-meter free and four in the 200-meter fly.

Personal

Ugur's family moved to the United States from Turkey when he was just seven months old, and he now holds dual citizenship. He is married to Liesl Kolbisen Taner, who is an impressive swimmer in her own right. She won U.S. championships in both the 100-meter free (1996, 1999) and 50-meter free (1999). The couple has three children: Brooks, Channing and Vaughn. Ugur plays lead electric guitar for Christian artist Matt Nightingale (www.mattnightingal.net). He also loves Texas barbeque! Ugur is the audio/video director at Peninsula Covenant Church in Redwood City, California.

Spiritual

Ugur's heart was convicted while listening to Pastor Tommy Nelson's powerful series "Song of Solomon." He credits much of his spiritual growth to Greg Rhodenbaugh, assistant coach at the University of Arizona.

Krystal Thomas

Birthday: June 10, 1989
Birthplace: Orlando, FL
Height: 6' 4"
Sport: Basketball
College: Duke University
Olympics: 2012 Olympic hopeful

Krystal hopes to qualify for the 2012 U.S. Olympic women's basketball team. In her first season at Duke, she's excited about progressing as a player. Even though Duke has made it to the Final Four in four of the last nine seasons, they haven't won a national championship. And that's something Krystal hopes to change in the near future. After her college career, she would like to go on to play in the WNBA.

Career

After one of the most decorated prep basketball careers in Florida history, Krystal got a taste of gold when she led the USA U-19 World Championship team to a 9-0 record and the gold medal in Bratis-lava, Slovakia. At the First Academy under Coach Steve Murray, Krys-tal led her team to two state championships. Her senior year she amassed 24 double-doubles, completing 61.6 percent of her field goals. Her honors include USA Parade All-American team, McDonald's All-Americans, Miss Florida Basketball, Florida Gatorade Player of the Year and nominee for National Gatorade Player of the Year.

Personal

Krystal describes herself as "driven." Although she was thrilled to be invited to try out for the U.S. National Basketball team, she missed her First Academy graduation to audition. "My school surprised me by holding a special graduation ceremony during our team banquet, presenting me with my diploma and retiring my jersey, #34." Krystal has always been gifted academically, maintaining a 3.99 G.P.A. She enjoys public speaking and was student body president her senior year.

Favorite Tune

"No Weapon" by Fred Hammond

Spiritual

If she wrote an autobiography, she would entitle it, *Krystal Thomas: Rising Above the Storm Called Life.* Krystal's faith remained strong even after her dad went to prison and her mom died of cancer.

Favorite Scripture Verses

Romans 8:31: "If God is for us, who can be against us?"

Philippians 3:13: "I do not consider myself yet to have taken hold of it. But one thing I do: Forgetting what is behind and straining toward what is ahead, I press on toward the goal to win the prize for which God has called me heavenward in Christ Jesus."

2 Timothy 4:7: "I have fought the good fight, I have finished the race, I have kept the faith."

Giving Back

Krystal helped raise her four siblings. She enjoyed visiting the Ronald McDonald House and seeing "faces lighting up" because of her team's presence. Since she was young, Krystal has dreamed of becoming a doctor.

Peter Westbrook

Birthday: April 16, 1952
Birthplace: Newark, NJ
Height: 5′ 9″
Sport: Fencing
College: New York University
Olympics: Six-time Olympian in fencing; 1984 Olympic bronze medalist in men's saber

Favorite Moment at the Games

"Los Angeles in 1984 was my favorite Olympics. It was run professionally and was very organized." In 1984, Peter won the bronze medal in men's saber. It was the first Olympic fencing medal won by an American since 1960.

Career

Peter won three gold medals in six Pan American Games. He continued fencing while becoming a top corporate salesman. A 13-time national champion in men's saber, Westbrook was inducted into the USFA Hall of Fame in 1996.

Personal

His book, *Harnessing Anger*, chronicles his fascinating life story from poverty and juvenile delinquency in Newark to a life of influence. In his 1976 debut at the Games, Peter tore a ligament in his leg and still managed to place in the top 13. Peter made the 1980 Olympic team, but he competed in China for three weeks instead due to the U.S. boycott of the Olympics.

Spiritual

Peter was raised Catholic and served in the choir and as an altar boy. However, he didn't start pursuing God until 1984. "Now the Lord is

No. 1 in my life. Every day I live to serve God. I'm always asking Him to transform me so I can be a better servant. I read the Scriptures more."

Giving Back
When he used his own money to start the Peter Westbrook Foundation in 1991, he never dreamed of the impact he would have. He attracted the attention of *60 Minutes, Fox News* and *People Magazine.* Four of his students have gone on to compete in the Games and are also helping him mentor other troubled kids into model citizens. Oprah Winfrey honored Peter with her Lifetime Achievement Award for his inspiration to thousands of inner-city youth. Peter also enjoys visiting the sick and encouraging the homeless. Check out his website at: www.peterwestbrook.org.

Cat Reddick Whitehill

Birthday: February 10, 1982
Birthplace: Richmond, VA
Height: 5' 7"
Sport: Soccer
College: University of North Carolina
Olympics: 2004 U.S. soccer team gold medalist

Favorite Olympic Moment
Defeating Brazil 2-1 in the gold medal match at the 2004 Olympic Games.

Career
From winning four consecutive high school state championships and two NCAA Championships to scoring two goals in the 2003 World Cup and leading Team USA to a gold medal at the 2004 Olympics, Cat Whitehill is a proven winner at every level of competitive soccer. A member of the 2007 World Cup team that won a bronze medal, Cat has scored 11 goals in international play. She has been a member of the U.S. Na-tional Team since 2000, playing in over 100 international matches. At the University of North Carolina, she proved to be the best defender in college soccer. As a member of two NCAA Championship teams, including a perfect 27-0 record her senior season, she was also named Final

Four Defensive MVP during both title runs. As a freshman, Cat also scored the game-winning goal against UCLA in the National Championship game. She became the twelfth player to have her jersey retired at UNC.

Personal
Cat's father played college football at Virginia Tech. She is a big college football fan. Cat loves to sing in her car, even though she admits she's not very good. She is also pursuing a broadcasting career.

Spiritual
"A lot of people would think sports would be a way of displeasing God. But I look at it as every day my way of worship. On game day, I look at the field as a kind of sanctuary to worship God."

Favorite Scripture Verse
Psalm 3:3: "But you are a shield around me, O LORD; you bestow glory on me and lift up my head."

Giving Back
Cat joined legendary Billie Jean King to speak to Congress on the topic of Title IX. "I do have a passion for women being able to play in any kind of sport on any kind of stage whether it be college, youth or professional."

Laura Wilkinson

Birthday: November 17, 1977
Birthplace: Houston, TX
Height: 5' 6"
Sports: Diving and Synchronized Diving
College: University of Texas
Olympics: 2000 U.S. Olympic gold medalist in 10-meter platform diving; 2004, 2008 U.S. Olympic diving team

Favorite Moment at the Games
"Standing on the podium receiving the gold medal was my favorite moment, although I'll never forget the moment right before my last

dive in Sydney." Laura was voted Best Female Athlete at the 2000 Olympics after she won the gold, upsetting the Chinese, despite her foot injury. It was the first time that an American woman had won a gold medal in platform diving since 1964. Her enthusiasm also earned her the 2000 U.S. Olympic Spirit Award.

Career

Called "tiger of the tower" by *Sports Illustrated*, Laura was a gymnast before she first tried diving at age 15. She was the only American diver, male or female, to win the gold medal at the Goodwill Games. And she's the only woman platform diver in history to ever earn a gold medal at the Olympics, World Cup and World Championships. Coached by Kenny Armstrong and Matt Scoggin, Laura won 17 U.S.A. Diving National titles (10 individual and 7 synchronized).

Personal

Her biggest thrill since winning the gold medal was getting married to the man she loves: her best friend, Eriek Hulseman! Wheaties prominently featured her on the cover and back of their cereal box.

Favorite Tune

"Big Enough" by Ayiesha Woods

Spiritual

"At the 1998 Goodwill Games in New York, I asked Josh Davis to pray for me. In the middle of that meet, I rededicated my life to God. I love to dive, I enjoy it, and I want to win, but that's not why I do it. It's to glorify God."

Favorite Scripture Verse

Philippians 4:13: "I can do everything through him who gives me strength."

Giving Back

Laura loves sharing with young teen girls on the Revolve Tour by Women of Faith (www.revolvetour.com). "Revolve has helped me come out of my shell. It's such a joy to see these young girls." Check out her website: www.laurawilkinson.com.

Gabe Woodward

Birthday: July 26, 1979
Birthplace: Bakersfield, CA
Height: 6' 2"
Sport: Swimming
College: University of Southern California
Olympics: 2004 U.S. Olympic bronze medalist in 400-meter freestyle relay

Favorite Moment at the Games

"Just before we walked out to the starting blocks, I looked at my relay teammates and said 'Guys, we are at the Olympics.' Gary Hall (five-time Olympic gold medalist and anchor on our relay) said, 'Yeah, we know, Gabe.' I said, 'Yeah, but I want you to know that I know that we are at the Olympics, so let's have some fun.'"

Career

Gabe was a four-time All-American while attending the University of Southern California and served as team co-captain his senior year. While competing at the World University Games in 1999, he earned a bronze medal in the 400-meter freestyle relay. He swam a great leg for the 400-meter freestyle relay team in the preliminaries at the 2004 Olympic Games that helped the United States claim the bronze medal. Gabe won silver and bronze at the 2007 Pan American Games and is preparing for the 2008 Olympic team.

Personal

Gabe has been married for five years to his beautiful wife, Staci. They have a daughter, Reese, who is three years old, and a son, Hudson, who is a year old. Gabe is an assistant vice president for Bank of America as a financial advisor.

Spiritual

Gabe grew up in a Christian home and has been a key leader for Swimmer's Chapel for many years.

Giving Back

Currently Gabe is a volunteer assistant coach with California State University of Bakersfield Men's Swim Team.

Special Thanks

This book wouldn't have been possible without my fellow Olympians allowing me to interview them and to find out how God has demonstrated His love to them. To all my coaches who brought me to this place: Eddie Reese, Kris Kubik, Randy Reese, Al Marks, Jim Yates and Jack Roach. And to Fletcher Watson, thanks for being the first to believe.

To my mom and dad, Joan and Mike Davis: I couldn't have asked for more love or a better childhood. Thanks for helping me get started in swimming and in life! To my siblings, Sam, Will and Tynan. And, Sam, a special thanks for your help on this book. It's great to watch you in your sweet spot.

To all my extended family, thanks for making me a very blessed nephew, cousin and in-law. I cherish the love you have given me.

Darlene and Donnie Cornelius, John Cornelius, Casey and Danielle Bookout, thanks for all your time, labor and love. And, Casey, thanks for helping with this book. You hit another home run!

To my pastor, Max Lucado: I might swim faster, but you sure take the gold in book writing. Thanks for your inspiration and super teaching. I appreciate our family and friends at Oak Hills Community Church.

I'm eternally grateful to my spiritual coaches: Darin McFarland (AIA), Craig Harriman (AIA), Geoff Warner (AIA), Ron Rogers (FCA), Rob Harrell and Chad McMillan. Ashley Null, your faithfulness has been a wonderful example to me of God's faithfulness. Thank you for your contributions to this book and, more importantly, to my life.

Evan Morganstein, God used you to extend my career 10 years longer than anybody thought possible. It has been a privilege to learn from you and laugh with you. Your support and friendship have been invaluable!

A special thanks to my teammates and friends who came alongside my journey and made it fun to pursue excellence: Kit Patterson, Todd Hargrove, Jonathan Jennings, Jason Patrick, Scott James, Eric Allen, Nate Thompson, Shae McCowan, Ugur Taner, Matt Domin, Todd Laurie, Jason French, Roger Borbon, Gary Hall, Jr., Brad Schumacher and Murray Easton.

Thanks to the individual and corporate sponsors who helped make my dream to be an Olympian a reality: The Nath family, Fred O'Connor, James Allen, Jim Lienenger, Red McCombs, Speedo, Splash Super Pools, Swimways, Auro-Dri, The Walker Family, Oroweat, and Bank of America. And a special thanks to Mutual of Omaha: Thank you for believing in me and giving me an opportunity to represent you.

Steven Lawson, you're the best editor! Regal Books—Mark Weising, Aly Hawkins and Rob Williams—thanks for giving me this opportunity. To Jay Carty, John Naber and Corey Cleek, thanks for your help getting this project launched.

Julie Martinez, you were a blessing! Roxanne Robbins (our "B.P." friend), a big thanks to you for opening doors I couldn't open. Rick Rupard and Pat Weiss, your help proofreading was greatly appreciated.

Also special thanks to Karen Hill, Adam McManus, Amy Hammond Hagberg, Marty Melle, Pat Williams, Mary Ford with Goodwin Sports Management, Mark Sweeney, Julie Abel, Susan Duke, Sherry Deluzio, Dwight Bain, Shelly Ballestero, Jeff Carrine, Mary Ellen Murray, Nancy Knowles, Amy Jamerson and Michelle Workman. Lore Jimienez, blessings for going beyond the call of duty and serving without being asked as we wrote.

And to my beautiful wife, Shantel. Thanks for helping, once again, to make everything better. To my children, Caleb, Abby, Luke,

Annie and Liam—you light up my life. Thanks for sacrificing our summer vacation so that I could write this book.

And a very special thanks to LeAnn Weiss! LeAnn, I'm glad we are all going to live forever so that I can have plenty of opportunities to say thank you for all you've done to make this book possible. You are the Encouragement Lady!

About John Ashley Null

I first met Ashley at the chaplaincy center in the Athletes' Village at the 1991 World University Games in Sheffield, England. I was immediately at ease because I could tell he couldn't care less about how fast or famous I was. It was evident that Ashley genuinely cared about my spiritual well-being and growth. He encouraged me and prayed for me at that swimming competition, and he's done that every meet since then for the last 17 years.

Helping athletes become mature Christians is clearly one of Ashley's great passions. He has served as an official chaplain at major international sports events since 1982, including both the 1984 and 2004 Olympic Games.

In addition to sports chaplaincy, Ashley is also an internationally respected expert on the English Reformation. He holds a BA from SMU, two advanced degrees from Yale and a PhD from Cambridge, England. He currently serves as the Canon Theologian of the Episcopal Diocese of Western Kansas and works with Caritas, a ministry that provides chaplaincies for world-class sporting events. Because of his unique blend of deep scholarly learning and practical pastoral insights, Ashley is a sought-after writer and speaker for the Anglican community around the globe as well as many universities.

I can testify to Ashley's pastoral wisdom. His writings and encouragement have been key to numerous "God moments" in my life. This is especially true of his book *Real Joy: Freedom to Be Your Best*, on how to be a Christian athlete in today's complicated world. *Real Joy* is, in my opinion, the most insightful and concise communiqué on how Jesus frees us from our enemies and obstacles so that we can be at our very best.

If you know anyone age 12 or older who is involved in sports, this would make an excellent gift book. I would also highly recommend it for use in small-group studies and as a great resource for athlete chapel outreaches. Don't be left out—find out how you can experience real joy in your sport and life today!

Josh Davis

Josh Davis Contact Information

Since 1997, Josh Davis has been cofounder of the largest swim clinic in the country, USA Swim Clinics. Josh visits approximately 100 cities a year, teaching swimming, inspiring kids at schools, motivating civic and corporate groups, and encouraging youth groups and churches. If you would like Josh to visit your community, please send an email to joshdavis@usaswimmer.com, or call (210) 494-9671.